Crafting Games with Python & Pygame: Game Development Unleashed

Kameron Hussain and Frahaan Hussain

Published by Sonar Publishing, 2024.

While every precaution has been taken in the preparation of this book, the publisher assumes no responsibility for errors or omissions, or for damages resulting from the use of the information contained herein.

CRAFTING GAMES WITH PYTHON & PYGAME: GAME DEVELOPMENT UNLEASHED

First edition. October 13, 2024.

Copyright © 2024 Kameron Hussain and Frahaan Hussain.

ISBN: 979-8227461551

Written by Kameron Hussain and Frahaan Hussain.

Crafting Games with Python & PYGAME

Game Development Unleashed

FIRST EDITION

Table of Contents

Preface

Game development has become one of the most exciting and rapidly evolving fields of software engineering. With advancements in technology and accessibility, more individuals are stepping into this creative domain to build their own games, whether for fun, education, or professional aspirations. The tools for game creation have expanded, but one particularly powerful and accessible toolset for beginners is Python combined with the Pygame library.

This book aims to provide a comprehensive introduction to game development using Python and Pygame, two technologies that have made creating 2D games more approachable than ever. Whether you are an experienced Python programmer or someone just starting out, this book will guide you through the essential concepts and techniques necessary to develop interactive, engaging games.

Starting from the basics of Python programming and an introduction to Pygame, we'll take you on a journey from drawing your first game window to developing complex games with sound, physics, and even multiplayer functionality. Along the way, you will gain insight into topics such as handling user input, managing game assets, and creating polished, responsive gameplay experiences.

As game development involves various disciplines such as graphics, sound, and logic, this book will touch on all these areas, giving you a rounded perspective on what it takes to create a complete game. Each chapter introduces new concepts and challenges, with examples and exercises designed to help you practice and solidify your understanding.

By the end of this book, you will not only have the knowledge to build your own games from scratch but also be well-equipped to explore more advanced topics in game development, whether using Pygame or transitioning to other game development frameworks. The skills you develop here will provide a solid foundation for all your future projects in the world of game development.

Happy coding and game-making!

Chapter 1: Introduction to Game Development

Understanding Game Development

Game development is a broad and dynamic field that encompasses many different skills, from programming and logic design to art, sound, and storytelling. At its core, however, game development is about creating an interactive experience for players. In modern game development, various game engines and frameworks simplify the process by providing pre-built systems for rendering graphics, handling input, and managing game assets.

Developing a game requires thinking about both the technical and creative aspects. The technical side includes writing the code that governs the behavior of the game, while the creative side involves designing characters, levels, sound effects, and more. Striking a balance between these two facets is key to producing a successful game.

For beginner developers, the process of creating games might seem overwhelming, but breaking it down into manageable steps makes it much more achievable. Python is an excellent language to start with due to its simplicity and readability. It also boasts a rich ecosystem of libraries, including Pygame, which is designed for writing games in Python.

Pygame is a set of Python modules designed for writing video games. It provides functionality for creating windows, handling user input, rendering images, and playing sounds, among other things. With Pygame, even a small amount of code can yield a working game prototype.

When learning game development, it is important to start with small projects. Begin by creating something simple, like a Pong game or a basic platformer, and gradually add complexity as you learn new skills. By iterating on your ideas and prototypes, you can develop a deeper understanding of how to structure and optimize your games.

Game development also involves an iterative process. Often, developers will create a prototype, test it, refine it, and repeat the cycle until the game achieves the desired level of polish. This workflow is essential for fixing bugs, enhancing gameplay, and making sure the game is fun for players.

One of the most exciting aspects of game development is the sense of creativity and problem-solving it encourages. You'll constantly face challenges that require you to think outside the box, whether you're designing a new game mechanic or optimizing performance for a better user experience. With Python and Pygame, you have the tools to bring your game ideas to life.

Lastly, community involvement is a significant part of game development. Many developers participate in game jams—competitions where teams create games over a short period of time—or share their projects online for feedback. This collaborative spirit helps developers learn from each other, improve their craft, and stay motivated.

Overview of Python and Pygame

Python is a versatile, high-level programming language known for its ease of use and readability. It is widely used in various fields such as web development, data analysis, artificial intelligence, and, of course, game development. The simplicity of Python makes it a great language for beginners, while its extensive libraries and active community make it a powerful tool for experienced developers.

In the context of game development, Python's role is to serve as the core scripting language for building game logic, handling player inputs, and managing other game systems. Combined with Pygame, it becomes a lightweight yet efficient platform for developing 2D games. Pygame is built on top of SDL (Simple DirectMedia Layer), which allows it to handle graphics, sounds, and other multimedia tasks seamlessly.

One of the benefits of using Python for game development is its strong focus on readability and code clarity. Unlike languages such as C++ or Java, which can have steep learning curves due to their syntax and memory management requirements, Python allows you to focus more on the logic and design of your game without being bogged down by technical details.

Pygame is an open-source library that simplifies many of the tasks required for game development. It provides modules for creating windows, drawing shapes, loading images, and managing audio. It also handles game-specific tasks like detecting keyboard and mouse inputs, managing game loops, and handling basic physics.

To give a brief example of Pygame in action, here's how you would create a simple game window:

```python
import pygame

# Initialize Pygame

pygame.init()

# Set up the game window

screen = pygame.display.set_mode((640, 480))
pygame.display.set_caption('My First Pygame Window')

# Main game loop
```

```
running = True

while running:

for event in pygame.event.get():

if event.type == pygame.QUIT:

running = False

# Quit the game

pygame.quit()
```

This code demonstrates how to create a basic game window that stays open until the user closes it. The pygame.display.set_mode() function sets the size of the window, and pygame.display.set_caption() changes the window's title. The game loop listens for events, such as the user closing the window, and exits the game when necessary.

Pygame makes it easy to start small and expand your project over time. As you progress through this book, you'll see how Pygame can be used to build increasingly complex games with advanced features like sound, animations, and physics.

Python and Pygame also offer flexibility for developers. Whether you're developing for fun, learning purposes, or even commercial projects, these tools provide a robust foundation for game development. Plus, they are cross-platform, allowing you to create games that run on Windows, macOS, and Linux without significant changes to your code.

Finally, as a beginner, you'll appreciate Python's large community and wealth of resources, including tutorials, forums, and open-source projects. These resources are invaluable as you navigate your way through the challenges of game development.

Setting Up Your Development Environment

Before diving into actual game development, it's crucial to set up your development environment properly. Having a functional setup allows you to focus on coding and building games rather than troubleshooting issues with your environment. The steps for setting up your environment are fairly straightforward, especially for Python and Pygame.

The first step is to install Python. You can download Python from the official Python website (python.org). It's important to ensure that you are using a version of Python that is compatible with Pygame, which is generally any version of Python 3.x. The installation process is simple: download the installer for your operating system and follow the prompts. Make sure to check the box that adds Python to your system's PATH during the installation process.

Next, you'll need to install Pygame. Pygame can be easily installed via pip, Python's package manager. Open a terminal or command prompt and run the following command:

```
pip install pygame
```

This command will download and install the latest version of Pygame from the Python Package Index (PyPI). Once the installation is complete, you can verify that Pygame is installed correctly by opening a Python shell and typing the following:

```
import pygame

print(pygame.ver)
```

If Pygame is installed correctly, this command will display the version of Pygame that you have installed. If you encounter any issues, the

Pygame documentation provides troubleshooting tips and guidance for resolving common installation problems.

Once Python and Pygame are installed, it's a good idea to set up a code editor or integrated development environment (IDE) for writing your code. Popular code editors for Python development include Visual Studio Code, Sublime Text, and Atom. For a more feature-rich experience, you can use an IDE like PyCharm, which offers advanced features such as code completion, debugging, and integrated version control.

Your development environment should also include tools for version control, such as Git. Version control allows you to track changes to your code over time, collaborate with others, and roll back to previous versions if necessary. GitHub is a popular platform for hosting Git repositories and sharing your code with others.

Finally, setting up a good file structure for your game projects is important for keeping your code organized. A typical file structure for a Pygame project might look like this:

my_game/

assets/

images/

sounds/

src/

main.py

player.py

enemy.py

README.md

requirements.txt

In this structure, the assets folder contains images, sounds, and other game resources, while the src folder contains the Python source code for the game. Keeping your assets and code separate helps maintain clarity and organization as your project grows.

Now that your environment is set up, you're ready to start building your first game!

First Steps: Your First Pygame Window

Creating your first Pygame window is a significant milestone in your journey as a game developer. It might seem like a simple task, but it represents the foundation upon which all other game components will be built. Your game's window is where all the action takes place, from rendering graphics to handling user input.

Pygame makes it easy to create a basic window with just a few lines of code. Here's how to do it:

```python
import pygame

# Initialize Pygame

pygame.init()

# Set up the game window

screen = pygame.display.set_mode((640, 480))

pygame.display.set_caption('My First Game')

# Main game loop
```

```python
running = True

while running:

    for event in pygame.event.get():

        if event.type == pygame.QUIT:

            running = False

# Quit the game

pygame.quit()
```

This script initializes Pygame, creates a window with a size of 640x480 pixels, and sets the window title to "My First Game." The game loop keeps the window open until the player closes it.

In Pygame, the window is represented by the screen object, which is created by calling pygame.display.set_mode(). The size of the window is defined by a tuple representing the width and height in pixels. In this case, we're using a 640x480 window, which is a common size for 2D games.

The pygame.display.set_caption() function sets the title of the window. You can customize this string to reflect the name of your game.

The main game loop is the heart of any game. It repeatedly checks for events (such as keyboard or mouse input) and updates the game state accordingly. In this example, the game loop listens for the QUIT event, which is triggered when the player clicks the close button on the window. When this event is detected, the game sets running to False, exiting the loop and closing the window.

It's important to understand that the game loop is where all the action happens in a game. In future sections, you'll learn how to use the game loop to handle input, update game logic, and render graphics. But for now, you've successfully created your first game window.

Once your window is up and running, you can begin adding other elements, such as images, sound effects, and animations. Pygame provides all the tools you need to turn this simple window into a fully functional game.

Chapter 2: Python Basics for Game Development

Python Fundamentals

Python is a versatile programming language that is particularly well-suited for beginners because of its readable syntax and powerful libraries. Understanding the basic structure and features of Python is essential for game development, especially when working with frameworks like Pygame. In this section, we will cover the fundamental aspects of Python that you need to get started with game development.

At its core, Python is an interpreted language, meaning that the code is executed line-by-line by the Python interpreter. This makes it easy to test, debug, and modify code quickly. The main building blocks of Python include variables, data types, and control flow structures.

Variables

Variables in Python are used to store data that can be referenced and manipulated later. Python allows for dynamic typing, meaning you don't need to declare the type of variable explicitly.

player_name = "Alex"

score = 0

In the example above, player_name is a string, and score is an integer. Python automatically infers the type based on the value assigned to the variable.

Control Flow

Control flow statements, such as if, else, and elif, help direct the flow of your program based on conditions.

if score > 100:

print("You won!")

else:

print("Keep playing!")

This is a basic conditional that prints different messages depending on the player's score. You can also use loops, such as for and while, to repeat tasks.

Functions

Functions are blocks of reusable code that perform a specific task. In Python, you can define a function using the def keyword.

def update_score(points):

global score

score += points

The function update_score takes in a parameter points and updates the global score variable.

By understanding these basic principles, you'll have a solid foundation for writing Python code in a game development environment.

Data Types and Structures

Data types and structures are fundamental to Python, enabling developers to organize and manipulate data effectively. Python offers several built-in data types, such as integers, floats, strings, and booleans. These types form the foundation for more complex data structures like lists, dictionaries, and tuples.

Integers and Floats

Integers (int) represent whole numbers, while floats (float) represent numbers with decimal points. These are commonly used in games to handle scores, positions, and other numeric values.

lives = 3

gravity = 9.8

In this example, lives is an integer, and gravity is a floating-point number.

Strings

Strings are sequences of characters enclosed in quotes. They are often used for storing player names, messages, and other text.

player_name = "Alex"

welcome_message = "Welcome to the game!"

Lists

Lists are ordered collections of items, and they can store multiple types of data. Lists are commonly used in games to store groups of objects like enemies, projectiles, or inventory items.

```
enemies = ["Goblin", "Orc", "Dragon"]
```

You can access individual items in a list using their index, starting from zero.

```
first_enemy = enemies[0] # Goblin
```

Dictionaries

Dictionaries store data in key-value pairs. In game development, dictionaries can be useful for storing attributes of game objects.

```
player = {

"name": "Alex",

"score": 0,

"lives": 3

}
```

You can access a value by referencing its key:

```
player_name = player["name"]
```

Tuples

Tuples are similar to lists, but they are immutable, meaning their contents cannot be changed after creation. Tuples are often used for fixed data like coordinates or settings.

```
screen_resolution = (800, 600)
```

By mastering Python's data types and structures, you will be able to efficiently manage and manipulate the data within your game.

Functions and Modules

Functions in Python allow you to encapsulate code into reusable blocks, making your programs more organized and modular. Functions are essential in game development for creating repetitive tasks, such as updating the game state, handling input, or rendering graphics.

Defining Functions

To define a function in Python, use the def keyword followed by the function name and any parameters. The body of the function contains the code that will be executed when the function is called.

```
def move_player(x, y):

player_position = (x, y)

return player_position
```

This function move_player takes two parameters, x and y, representing the player's coordinates on the screen. The function returns the updated position of the player.

Calling Functions

Once a function is defined, you can call it by using its name followed by parentheses and providing any necessary arguments.

```
new_position = move_player(100, 200)

print(new_position) # Output: (100, 200)
```

Return Values

Functions can return values that can be used later in the program. This is especially important in game development, where you might want to return game states, positions, or scores from a function.

```python
def calculate_score(base_score, bonus):

total_score = base_score + bonus

return total_score

final_score = calculate_score(100, 50)

print(final_score) # Output: 150
```

Modules

Modules are collections of Python functions and variables organized into a file. Pygame itself is a module that you'll import into your game to access its functions. You can create your own modules by organizing your game code into different files.

```python
import pygame

from my_game_functions import move_player, calculate_score
```

Here, we import both pygame and specific functions from a custom module my_game_functions.

Using functions and modules allows you to keep your code organized, reusable, and easy to maintain, which is crucial when developing more complex games.

Object-Oriented Programming in Python

Object-oriented programming (OOP) is a powerful paradigm in Python that allows you to model real-world entities as objects. In game development, OOP is especially useful because games often involve multiple entities, such as players, enemies, items, and levels, each with its own properties and behaviors.

Classes and Objects

In Python, a class is a blueprint for creating objects. Each object can have attributes (variables) and methods (functions) that define its behavior. To define a class, use the class keyword.

```
class Player:

def __init__(self, name, lives):

self.name = name

self.lives = lives

def lose_life(self):

self.lives -= 1
```

In the example above, we define a Player class with two attributes (name and lives) and a method (lose_life). The __init__ method is a special method in Python used to initialize the object's attributes.

Creating Objects

To create an object from a class, simply call the class as if it were a function:

```
player1 = Player("Alex", 3)
```

This creates a new Player object with the name "Alex" and 3 lives. You can then call the object's methods:

player1.lose_life()

print(player1.lives) # Output: 2

Inheritance

OOP also supports inheritance, which allows one class to inherit attributes and methods from another class. This is useful in games when you want to create specialized versions of a class, such as different types of enemies.

class Enemy(Player):

def __init__(self, name, lives, attack_power):

super().__init__(name, lives)

self.attack_power = attack_power

Here, the Enemy class inherits from the Player class but also adds a new attribute, attack_power.

Object-oriented programming is a powerful way to organize and structure your game code, making it more modular and easier to extend as your game grows in complexity.

Chapter 3: Introduction to Pygame

What is Pygame?

Pygame is a Python library designed specifically for writing video games. It provides functionalities like creating game windows, handling events, managing graphics, sounds, and more. Pygame is built on top of the Simple DirectMedia Layer (SDL), a low-level C library, which allows for fast and efficient multimedia handling, such as rendering images, sounds, and managing input devices.

One of the reasons Pygame is a popular choice for game development, especially for beginners, is its simplicity. Unlike more complex game development frameworks, Pygame provides all the basic tools you need to build simple 2D games without needing extensive knowledge of graphics or audio systems. Despite its simplicity, it is powerful enough to create relatively sophisticated games.

To get started with Pygame, you need to install it first. This can be done easily via pip, Python's package installer:

```
pip install pygame
```

Once installed, you can begin creating game windows, drawing shapes, playing sounds, and more.

Another major feature of Pygame is its ability to handle events. Games rely on continuous user input, like keyboard presses or mouse movements. Pygame allows you to manage this efficiently using its event system.

Here's an example of a simple Pygame window creation:

```
import pygame
```

```python
# Initialize Pygame

pygame.init()

# Set up the game window

screen = pygame.display.set_mode((800, 600))

pygame.display.set_caption('My First Pygame Window')

# Game loop

running = True

while running:

for event in pygame.event.get():

if event.type == pygame.QUIT:

running = False

screen.fill((0, 0, 0)) # Fill the screen with black

pygame.display.flip() # Update the display

# Quit Pygame

pygame.quit()
```

This code initializes Pygame, sets up a window of size 800x600, and enters a game loop that keeps the window open until the user closes it.

Pygame has many built-in functions to handle input devices like keyboards, mice, and joysticks. Additionally, it supports loading, displaying, and transforming images, making it ideal for 2D game development.

Although Pygame is primarily used for creating 2D games, you can still develop complex projects with rich game mechanics and design. It is also a good stepping stone to more advanced game development libraries.

In summary, Pygame is a great tool for learning game development. It is simple, efficient, and suitable for building a wide range of 2D games. Whether you want to build a classic arcade-style game, an RPG, or a simple puzzle game, Pygame provides all the tools you need to get started.

Installing and Configuring Pygame

Before you can begin creating games with Pygame, you need to ensure that your development environment is properly set up. This includes installing Python, setting up Pygame, and ensuring that everything is configured correctly.

First, make sure that you have Python installed on your computer. If you don't have Python yet, you can download and install it from the official Python website. Once Python is installed, you can install Pygame using pip. Here's the command you would run in your terminal:

```
pip install pygame
```

This will download and install the Pygame library, along with any dependencies. Once Pygame is installed, you can check that everything is working by running a simple script. Create a new Python file and add the following code:

```
import pygame

# Initialize Pygame
```

```python
pygame.init()

# Set up a window with a title

screen = pygame.display.set_mode((640, 480))

pygame.display.set_caption('Pygame Test Window')

# Main loop

running = True

while running:

for event in pygame.event.get():

if event.type == pygame.QUIT:

running = False

# Quit Pygame

pygame.quit()
```

Run this script, and you should see a blank window with the title "Pygame Test Window." This confirms that Pygame is installed and running correctly.

If you encounter any issues, it might be due to conflicts between Python versions or dependencies. In such cases, using a virtual environment can help isolate your Python and Pygame installation. You can create a virtual environment using the following commands:

```
python -m venv mygameenv

source mygameenv/bin/activate # On Windows use: mygameenv\Scripts\activate
```

After activating the environment, install Pygame again using pip within the virtual environment.

For development, many IDEs like PyCharm, VS Code, and others work seamlessly with Python and Pygame. They provide features such as code completion, debugging tools, and integrated terminal access, which can significantly speed up your development process.

Once Pygame is installed and your environment is set up, you are ready to start developing games. Your first task will likely involve creating a game window, managing events, and building your game loop.

In addition to window management, Pygame provides support for rendering graphics, playing sounds, handling input, and more. You can explore the extensive Pygame documentation to learn more about its capabilities.

Pygame Basics: Creating a Game Window

Creating a game window in Pygame is the first step toward building any game. The game window is the canvas on which you will draw your game's graphics, display information to the player, and respond to user input.

To create a basic window in Pygame, you first need to initialize the library, create the window, and set up a game loop. The game loop is responsible for continuously updating the game state and rendering the graphics. Here is a minimal example:

```
import pygame

# Initialize Pygame

pygame.init()

# Set up the display (width, height)
```

```python
screen = pygame.display.set_mode((800, 600))

# Set the window title

pygame.display.set_caption('Pygame Game Window')

# Main game loop

running = True

while running:

for event in pygame.event.get():

if event.type == pygame.QUIT:

running = False

# Fill the screen with white

screen.fill((255, 255, 255))

# Update the display

pygame.display.flip()

# Quit Pygame

pygame.quit()
```

In this script, we first initialize Pygame using pygame.init(). This is necessary to set up all the modules provided by Pygame. Next, we create the game window using pygame.display.set_mode(). The parameters passed to this function define the window size, in this case, 800 pixels wide and 600 pixels tall.

After setting the window's title using pygame.display.set_caption(), we enter the game loop. The game loop is essential for any game, as it allows the game to continuously process user input, update the game state, and render graphics to the screen. In this example, we handle the pygame.QUIT event, which is triggered when the user attempts to close the window.

Inside the game loop, we also use screen.fill() to fill the window with a color, in this case, white (255, 255, 255). Finally, we call pygame.display.flip() to update the display with the new content.

This simple setup can be expanded to include game logic, rendering of sprites and images, handling input, and more.

Event Handling and Game Loop

The game loop is a critical concept in any game. It is responsible for updating the game's state, processing user input, and rendering graphics on the screen. The loop runs continuously while the game is active, usually many times per second, ensuring smooth gameplay.

In Pygame, event handling is done using pygame.event.get(), which retrieves all the events that have occurred since the last call to the function. Events can include user actions like pressing keys, moving the mouse, or closing the window. Here's an example of handling multiple types of input:

import pygame

Initialize Pygame

pygame.init()

Create a window

screen = pygame.display.set_mode((640, 480))

Main game loop

```python
running = True

while running:

    for event in pygame.event.get():

        if event.type == pygame.QUIT:

            running = False

        elif event.type == pygame.KEYDOWN:

            if event.key == pygame.K_SPACE:

                print("Space key pressed!")

        elif event.type == pygame.MOUSEBUTTONDOWN:

            print(f"Mouse button clicked at {event.pos}")

    screen.fill((0, 0, 0))

    pygame.display.flip()

pygame.quit()
```

In this example, we handle three types of events: quitting the game, pressing the spacebar, and clicking the mouse. This illustrates how you can respond to different types of input in your game.

The game loop is where you will implement most of your game logic. It should be optimized for performance, as it will be called repeatedly during gameplay.

Chapter 4: Graphics and Images

Drawing Shapes and Text

In Pygame, drawing shapes and text on the screen is an essential aspect of creating visual elements for games. Pygame provides several functions to draw simple geometric shapes such as rectangles, circles, and lines. These functions are part of the pygame.draw module, which allows you to customize the color, thickness, and position of these shapes.

The basic process for drawing shapes involves the following steps:

1. Create a surface (usually the game window).
2. Use pygame.draw functions to draw shapes on the surface.
3. Update the display to reflect the changes.

Here's an example of drawing a simple rectangle and a circle on the screen:

```
import pygame

# Initialize Pygame

pygame.init()

# Set up the display

screen = pygame.display.set_mode((800, 600))

# Set up color

white = (255, 255, 255)

blue = (0, 0, 255)
```

```python
# Main loop

running = True

while running:

    for event in pygame.event.get():

        if event.type == pygame.QUIT:

            running = False

    # Fill the screen with white color

    screen.fill(white)

    # Draw a rectangle (x, y, width, height)

    pygame.draw.rect(screen, blue, (100, 100, 200, 100))

    # Draw a circle (x, y, radius)

    pygame.draw.circle(screen, blue, (400, 300), 50)

    # Update the display

    pygame.display.flip()

pygame.quit()
```

In this code, the pygame.draw.rect() function is used to draw a blue rectangle, and pygame.draw.circle() draws a blue circle. The screen is updated each frame using pygame.display.flip().

Text rendering in Pygame requires creating a font object using pygame.font.Font(). Once you have a font object, you can render text by using the render() method. Here's an example of rendering text on the screen:

```
# Create a font object

font = pygame.font.Font(None, 36)

# Render text

text = font.render('Hello, Pygame!', True, blue)

# Blit the text on the screen

screen.blit(text, (300, 200))
```

This code creates a font object with size 36 and renders the text "Hello, Pygame!" in blue.

By combining shapes and text, you can create user interfaces, HUDs, and other visual elements for your game.

Working with Images and Sprites

Handling images and sprites is a critical part of game development, as they form the visual representation of characters, objects, and backgrounds in the game. Pygame offers several ways to load, manipulate, and display images on the screen.

To load an image, you use the pygame.image.load() function. The image is then converted to a format suitable for display using the convert() or convert_alpha() methods. Once loaded, the image can be drawn on the screen using the blit() method.

Here's an example of loading and displaying an image:

```
import pygame
# Initialize Pygame
pygame.init()
```

```python
# Set up the display

screen = pygame.display.set_mode((800, 600))

# Load an image

image = pygame.image.load('player.png').convert_alpha()

# Main loop

running = True

while running:

for event in pygame.event.get():

if event.type == pygame.QUIT:

running = False

# Fill the screen with a color

screen.fill((255, 255, 255))

# Blit the image onto the screen at (100, 100)

screen.blit(image, (100, 100))

# Update the display

pygame.display.flip()

pygame.quit()
```

In this example, the convert_alpha() method is used because the image may have transparency. The blit() function is then used to draw the image on the screen at the specified position.

Sprites are objects that represent game entities, such as players or enemies. Pygame provides a pygame.sprite module to manage sprites more efficiently. A sprite class is created by inheriting from pygame.sprite.Sprite and implementing the necessary behavior, such as movement or animation.

Here's a basic sprite example:

```
class Player(pygame.sprite.Sprite):

def __init__(self):

super().__init__()

self.image = pygame.image.load('player.png').convert_alpha()

self.rect = self.image.get_rect()

def update(self):

# Update sprite logic (e.g., movement)

self.rect.x += 5
```

In this code, the Player class inherits from pygame.sprite.Sprite. The update() method is used to define the behavior of the sprite, such as movement or collision detection.

Using sprites helps in managing game objects in a structured way, especially when dealing with multiple objects like enemies or projectiles.

Managing Game Assets

Managing game assets, such as images, sounds, and fonts, is crucial for creating scalable and maintainable games. Pygame allows you to load and manage assets efficiently through various methods, including organizing assets in folders and creating asset managers.

It is a good practice to separate assets into distinct folders for images, sounds, and fonts. For example, you might have the following folder structure:

/assets

/images

/sounds

/fonts

You can load assets using relative paths, making it easier to manage them. For instance:

```
player_image = pygame.image.load('assets/images/player.png').convert_alpha()

jump_sound = pygame.mixer.Sound('assets/sounds/jump.wav')

font = pygame.font.Font('assets/fonts/arial.ttf', 36)
```

To further streamline asset management, you can create a custom asset manager class:

```
class AssetManager:

def __init__(self):

self.images = {}

self.sounds = {}

self.fonts = {}
```

```python
def load_image(self, name, path):

self.images[name] = pygame.image.load(path).convert_alpha()

def get_image(self, name):

return self.images.get(name)

def load_sound(self, name, path):

self.sounds[name] = pygame.mixer.Sound(path)

def get_sound(self, name):

return self.sounds.get(name)

def load_font(self, name, path, size):

self.fonts[name] = pygame.font.Font(path, size)

def get_font(self, name):

return self.fonts.get(name)
```

This AssetManager class helps load and retrieve assets using simple methods, keeping your game's codebase organized and efficient.

Animation Techniques

Animation in Pygame is accomplished by displaying a sequence of images (frames) over time. This is often used to animate characters, objects, or visual effects. The core concept is to change the image displayed in a sprite at regular intervals.

The simplest way to implement animation is to use a list of images and update the displayed image based on the game's frame count or a timer. Here's an example of a basic animation:

```python
class AnimatedSprite(pygame.sprite.Sprite):

def __init__(self, images):

super().__init__()

self.images = images

self.index = 0

self.image = self.images[self.index]

self.rect = self.image.get_rect()

def update(self):

# Update the animation by cycling through images

self.index += 1

if self.index >= len(self.images):

self.index = 0

self.image = self.images[self.index]
```

In this code, the AnimatedSprite class cycles through a list of images, updating the displayed image each frame. This creates the illusion of movement.

For more complex animations, such as handling different states (idle, walking, jumping), you can extend the AnimatedSprite class to manage different animation sequences.

```python
self.animations = {

'idle': [image1, image2],

'walk': [image3, image4, image5],
```

44

'jump': [image6]

}

Chapter 5: Handling Input

Keyboard Input

Keyboard input is one of the fundamental ways to control a game. In most games, players use the keyboard to move characters, interact with the environment, and perform actions. Pygame provides an easy-to-use interface for handling keyboard input through its event system.

Pygame captures all events such as key presses, mouse clicks, and system events in an event queue. To handle keyboard input, you need to check the event queue for KEYDOWN and KEYUP events. These events tell you when a key is pressed or released.

Here's an example of how to handle keyboard input in Pygame:

```python
import pygame

pygame.init()

# Set up the game window

screen = pygame.display.set_mode((640, 480))

running = True

while running:

for event in pygame.event.get():

if event.type == pygame.QUIT:

running = False

# Check for key presses

if event.type == pygame.KEYDOWN:
```

```python
if event.key == pygame.K_LEFT:

print("Left arrow key pressed")

if event.key == pygame.K_RIGHT:

print("Right arrow key pressed")

if event.key == pygame.K_ESCAPE:

running = False

pygame.quit()
```

In this example, KEYDOWN is used to detect when a key is pressed. Each key on the keyboard has a constant in Pygame that can be used to identify it (e.g., K_LEFT, K_RIGHT, K_ESCAPE). You can map these keys to specific actions in your game.

For continuous movement (e.g., holding down a key to move a character), it's better to check the state of the keys rather than relying on individual key events. Pygame provides the pygame.key.get_pressed() function for this purpose.

```python
import pygame

pygame.init()

screen = pygame.display.set_mode((640, 480))

clock = pygame.time.Clock()

running = True

while running:

for event in pygame.event.get():
```

```python
if event.type == pygame.QUIT:

running = False

keys = pygame.key.get_pressed()

if keys[pygame.K_LEFT]:

print("Moving left")

if keys[pygame.K_RIGHT]:

print("Moving right")

if keys[pygame.K_ESCAPE]:

running = False

pygame.display.flip()

clock.tick(60)

pygame.quit()
```

Here, pygame.key.get_pressed() returns a list of Boolean values representing the state of every key. If a key is pressed, its corresponding value in the list will be True.

Common Keyboard Controls in Games

In many games, the keyboard is used for character movement and interaction with the environment. For example, the arrow keys or WASD keys might be used for movement, while other keys (such as space for jumping or shift for running) handle additional actions. You can map these keys as per your game design.

```python
if keys[pygame.K_w]:
```

```python
    print("Move up")

if keys[pygame.K_a]:

    print("Move left")

if keys[pygame.K_s]:

    print("Move down")

if keys[pygame.K_d]:

    print("Move right")
```

For more complex games, you may need to create a custom input handler that maps multiple key combinations to different actions.

Key Combinations and Multiple Key Presses

Handling multiple key presses is essential for many games. For example, a player might want to move diagonally by pressing both K_LEFT and K_UP simultaneously. With the pygame.key.get_pressed() method, it's easy to check for multiple key presses.

```python
if keys[pygame.K_LEFT] and keys[pygame.K_UP]:

    print("Moving diagonally up-left")
```

Customizing Keyboard Controls

Many games allow players to customize their keyboard controls. This is typically done by providing a settings menu where players can remap keys to different actions. You can store the customized key mappings in a configuration file and load them at the start of the game.

Mouse Input

Mouse input is another common way to interact with a game. Pygame provides support for handling mouse events such as clicks, movement, and scrolling. Just like with keyboard input, Pygame captures mouse events in the event queue.

The main mouse events in Pygame are MOUSEBUTTONDOWN, MOUSEBUTTONUP, and MOUSEMOTION. MOUSEBUTTONDOWN and MOUSEBUTTONUP detect when a mouse button is pressed or released, while MOUSEMOTION detects movement of the mouse.

Here's an example of handling mouse clicks:

```python
import pygame

pygame.init()

screen = pygame.display.set_mode((640, 480))

running = True

while running:

for event in pygame.event.get():

if event.type == pygame.QUIT:

running = False

if event.type == pygame.MOUSEBUTTONDOWN:

if event.button == 1: # Left mouse button

print("Left mouse button clicked")

elif event.button == 3: # Right mouse button
```

```
print("Right mouse button clicked")
```

```
pygame.quit()
```

In this example, the event.button attribute is used to check which mouse button was pressed. The left mouse button is represented by 1, the right button by 3, and the middle button by 2.

You can also detect the position of the mouse when a button is clicked by accessing the event.pos attribute.

```
if event.type == pygame.MOUSEBUTTONDOWN:
```

```
print(f"Mouse clicked at {event.pos}")
```

Detecting Mouse Movement

Mouse movement is detected using the MOUSEMOTION event. This event is triggered whenever the mouse moves, and you can access the new position of the mouse through the event.pos attribute.

```
if event.type == pygame.MOUSEMOTION:
```

```
print(f"Mouse moved to {event.pos}")
```

In many games, you might want to detect when the mouse moves over a specific area (such as a button in a menu). You can use collision detection to check if the mouse coordinates overlap with a specific region.

Gamepad and Joystick Input

Gamepads and joysticks provide an alternative input method for games, especially for more complex games or those that benefit from analog controls. Pygame provides robust support for handling these devices through its joystick module.

Before you can handle gamepad input, you need to initialize the joystick subsystem:

```python
import pygame

pygame.init()

pygame.joystick.init()
```

After initializing the joystick, you can create a joystick object and start processing its events. First, you need to check how many joysticks are connected:

```python
joystick_count = pygame.joystick.get_count()

print(f"Number of joysticks: {joystick_count}")
```

Once you have a joystick, you can handle input events such as button presses, axis movement, and hat switches. Here's an example of handling button presses on a gamepad:

```python
joystick = pygame.joystick.Joystick(0)  # Use the first connected joystick

joystick.init()

while True:

for event in pygame.event.get():

if event.type == pygame.JOYBUTTONDOWN:

print(f"Button {event.button} pressed")
```

Analog Sticks and Axes

Most modern gamepads have analog sticks that return a continuous range of values, typically between -1.0 and 1.0. You can access these values through the get_axis() function:

x_axis = joystick.get_axis(0) # X-axis of the left stick

y_axis = joystick.get_axis(1) # Y-axis of the left stick

print(f"Left stick: ({x_axis}, {y_axis})")

Creating a Custom Input System

As games become more complex, it may become inefficient to handle each input event manually. A better approach is to create a custom input system that abstracts the handling of different input devices (keyboard, mouse, gamepad) and maps them to specific game actions.

For example, you can define a class InputHandler that listens for events and updates the state of various input devices:

class InputHandler:

def __init__(self):

self.keys = {}

self.mouse = {"left": False, "right": False}

self.joystick = None

def update(self):

for event in pygame.event.get():

if event.type == pygame.KEYDOWN:

```python
self.keys[event.key] = True

if event.type == pygame.KEYUP:

self.keys[event.key] = False

if event.type == pygame.MOUSEBUTTONDOWN:

if event.button == 1:

self.mouse["left"] = True

elif event.button == 3:

self.mouse["right"] = True

if event.type == pygame.MOUSEBUTTONUP:

if event.button == 1:

self.mouse["left"] = False

elif event.button == 3:

self.mouse["right"] = False
```

This class can be expanded to handle gamepad input as well. The benefit of using a custom input system is that it allows you to centralize input handling and make it easier to map different devices to the same actions in your game.

Chapter 6: Sound and Music

Introduction to Sound in Pygame

Sound is an essential component of game development. It enhances the gaming experience by adding depth and immersion, whether through background music, sound effects, or ambient sounds. Pygame provides a set of tools to incorporate audio into your game using the pygame.mixer module, which is responsible for all sound-related functions.

Before we can add sound, we need to ensure that pygame.mixer is initialized properly. This can be done by calling pygame.mixer.init() after initializing Pygame. The mixer module supports both music and sound effects, with distinct methods for handling each. Sound effects are short audio clips, while music is typically longer and looped.

Here's how you initialize pygame.mixer and load a sound effect:

import pygame

Initialize Pygame and mixer

pygame.init()

pygame.mixer.init()

Load a sound effect

sound_effect = pygame.mixer.Sound('path_to_sound.wav')

Play the sound effect

sound_effect.play()

The Sound class is used to load a sound file and create a sound object. You can call play() to trigger the sound, which will play asynchronously, meaning it won't block the rest of your game loop. You can also control volume, pause, and stop sounds with methods like set_volume() and stop().

For longer background music tracks, Pygame uses the pygame.mixer.music module. This handles streaming music from a file and offers different controls for managing playback, like looping.

Here's an example of loading and playing background music:

Load and play background music

pygame.mixer.music.load('background_music.mp3')

pygame.mixer.music.play(-1) # Loop indefinitely

The play() method's argument -1 tells the music to loop indefinitely. You can control the number of loops by adjusting this value. Setting it to 0 will play the music once, and higher numbers will loop that many times.

Keep in mind that sound and music files can impact your game's performance, so proper management of audio resources is essential. This involves pre-loading sounds where possible and ensuring efficient use of memory by limiting the number of active sound channels.

Adding Sound Effects

Sound effects are typically short, sharp sounds like gunshots, button clicks, or character footsteps. In Pygame, these are handled using the pygame.mixer.Sound class, which allows you to load and control sound effect files in your game.

The most common audio file formats used in Pygame are .wav and .ogg. Pygame provides support for these file types, but it's important to ensure your sound files are in a compatible format. Once your sound files are ready, you can load them into your game as Sound objects and trigger them at specific game events, such as when a player jumps or a projectile hits a target.

Here's an example of playing a sound effect when the player jumps:

jump_sound = pygame.mixer.Sound('jump.wav')

def player_jump():

jump_sound.play()

Handle jump logic here

You can further enhance your game's realism by controlling the volume of sound effects. The set_volume() method allows you to set a volume level between 0.0 (mute) and 1.0 (full volume).

jump_sound.set_volume(0.5) # Set the volume to 50%

In addition to adjusting volume, Pygame also allows you to pause or stop sound effects using the stop() method:

jump_sound.stop() # Stop the sound effect

Sound effects can overlap, and Pygame offers up to 8 sound channels by default. This means you can play multiple sound effects at once, but it's good practice to avoid overwhelming the player with too many simultaneous sounds. You can manage sound channels using pygame.mixer.set_num_channels() to adjust the number of concurrent sounds in your game.

Integrating Background Music

Background music is a key element in setting the mood and tone of your game. Whether it's an upbeat track for an action sequence or a somber melody for a dramatic moment, music can greatly influence how players perceive your game world.

In Pygame, background music is handled by the pygame.mixer.music module, which allows you to load and play longer music tracks. Unlike sound effects, background music is streamed from a file rather than fully loaded into memory, which is more efficient for longer tracks.

Here's an example of how to load and play background music:

```
pygame.mixer.music.load('background_music.mp3')
```

```
pygame.mixer.music.set_volume(0.6) # Set volume to 60%
```

```
pygame.mixer.music.play(-1) # Loop the music indefinitely
```

The play() method allows you to specify how many times the music should loop. Setting the loop value to -1 will play the music on an infinite loop, which is often desired for background music.

You can also pause, stop, or fade out the music. The fadeout() method is especially useful for transitioning between scenes smoothly:

```
pygame.mixer.music.fadeout(2000) # Fade out over 2 seconds
```

One key consideration when using background music is file size and format. Larger music files can slow down your game's loading time. Consider using compressed formats like .ogg or .mp3 to keep file sizes manageable without sacrificing audio quality.

Another important aspect is timing your music transitions. Pygame allows you to queue multiple music tracks, meaning one track can play immediately after the other ends:

pygame.mixer.music.queue('next_track.mp3')

This can be especially useful for games with multiple levels or dynamic music that changes based on player actions or game events.

Managing Audio Resources

Efficient management of audio resources is crucial to ensure your game runs smoothly. Mismanaging sound and music can lead to performance issues such as lag, delays in sound playback, or even crashes.

One way to optimize your game's performance is to limit the number of sound channels. Each sound effect in Pygame occupies a channel, and Pygame uses 8 channels by default. However, you can increase or decrease this number depending on the requirements of your game. For example:

pygame.mixer.set_num_channels(16) # Set 16 sound channels

It's also a good practice to pre-load sounds during your game's initialization phase. Loading sounds on the fly during gameplay can cause brief pauses or slowdowns, especially if your sound files are large. By pre-loading all necessary sound effects and music at the start of the game, you can avoid these issues.

Additionally, when a sound or music track is no longer needed, you should free up the memory by stopping the sound and releasing the resources. This is particularly important for games with complex soundscapes or large numbers of audio files.

Lastly, ensure that audio files are compressed and in a suitable format for your target platform. Different platforms may have different performance characteristics, and ensuring compatibility across systems will enhance the overall experience for your players.

Chapter 7: Game Physics and Collisions

Basics of Game Physics

Game physics is essential for creating realistic movements and interactions in video games. In the context of Pygame, physics can be implemented using custom algorithms, or by integrating libraries that handle physics simulations. At its core, game physics involves calculations related to motion, velocity, acceleration, and forces.

The primary concepts in game physics include:

1. **Velocity**: This represents the speed at which an object moves. Velocity is usually represented as a vector, which has both magnitude and direction.
2. **Acceleration**: Acceleration is the rate at which an object's velocity changes over time. When a player presses a key to move a character, the acceleration might increase, simulating a natural build-up of speed.
3. **Forces**: Forces such as gravity and friction affect how objects behave in the game. Gravity pulls objects down, while friction slows their motion when they come into contact with surfaces.
4. **Collisions**: Detecting and responding to collisions is crucial for interacting with the game world. When objects collide, they either bounce off, stop, or interact in other ways. Collision detection is usually performed using bounding boxes, circles, or polygons.

In Pygame, you can define physics using the game loop. By adjusting an object's position based on velocity and handling interactions like collisions, you can simulate physics.

```python
# Basic physics loop example in Pygame

player_pos = [100, 100]

player_vel = [2, 0] # Initial velocity

# Gravity constant

GRAVITY = 0.5

def update_physics():
# Apply gravity to vertical velocity

player_vel[1] += GRAVITY

# Update player position based on velocity

player_pos[0] += player_vel[0]

player_pos[1] += player_vel[1]
```

This example shows how velocity is updated with gravity and used to modify the player's position.

Implementing Gravity and Jump Mechanics

In platformer games, gravity and jumping mechanics are essential to player movement. Gravity pulls the player downward, while jumping propels the player upward. This creates a natural interaction with the environment.

To implement gravity, we apply a downward force to the player's vertical velocity each frame. For jumping, we apply an upward force when the player presses the jump button. The jump should only occur when the player is grounded (not in the air), preventing multiple jumps without landing.

Gravity Implementation

Gravity can be implemented by continuously adding a downward acceleration to the player's vertical velocity. This simulates the effect of gravity pulling the player down.

```python
# Gravity constant and velocity

GRAVITY = 0.8

player_vel = [0, 0] # Initial velocity

on_ground = False

def apply_gravity():

global player_vel, on_ground

if not on_ground:

player_vel[1] += GRAVITY # Apply gravity
```

In this code, gravity is applied to the vertical velocity of the player unless they are on the ground. The gravity constant can be adjusted to control the intensity of the gravitational force.

Jump Mechanics

To implement jumping, we need to modify the player's vertical velocity when the jump button is pressed. However, jumping should only be allowed when the player is on the ground to prevent unrealistic multiple jumps.

```python
JUMP_VELOCITY = -12 # Negative value to move upward

def jump():

global player_vel, on_ground
```

```python
if on_ground:

player_vel[1] = JUMP_VELOCITY # Apply upward velocity

on_ground = False
```

Here, when the player presses the jump button and is on the ground, an upward velocity is applied, launching the player into the air. The negative value represents upward movement.

Ground Detection

To prevent endless falling, it's essential to detect when the player is on the ground and stop further downward motion. Ground detection can be handled using collision detection with platforms or the game's floor.

```python
def check_ground():

global on_ground, player_pos, player_vel

if player_pos[1] >= FLOOR_HEIGHT: # If player hits the floor

on_ground = True

player_vel[1] = 0 # Stop downward velocity

player_pos[1] = FLOOR_HEIGHT # Reset position to floor level

else:

on_ground = False
```

This ensures the player stays grounded once they land, and their velocity is reset. You can adjust this method to detect ground for platforms or other surfaces.

Collision Detection and Response

Collision detection is a fundamental part of game physics, allowing objects to interact with one another and the game world. In Pygame, there are several methods to detect collisions, including bounding boxes, circles, and pixel-perfect collision detection. Once a collision is detected, the game must respond by altering the objects' positions or velocities.

Axis-Aligned Bounding Box (AABB) Collision Detection

One of the simplest and most widely used methods of collision detection is the Axis-Aligned Bounding Box (AABB). This technique checks whether the rectangles (bounding boxes) of two objects overlap.

```python
def check_collision(rect1, rect2):

if (rect1.x < rect2.x + rect2.width and

rect1.x + rect1.width > rect2.x and

rect1.y < rect2.y + rect2.height and

rect1.y + rect1.height > rect2.y):

return True

return False
```

In this code, rect1 and rect2 are the bounding boxes of two objects. The function returns True if the rectangles overlap.

Circle Collision Detection

For objects that are circular in shape, circle-based collision detection can be used. This method involves calculating the distance between two circles and comparing it with the sum of their radii.

```python
import math

def circle_collision(circle1, circle2):

    distance = math.sqrt((circle1.x - circle2.x)**2 + (circle1.y - circle2.y)**2)

    if distance < (circle1.radius + circle2.radius):

        return True

    return False
```

Here, the function calculates the Euclidean distance between the centers of two circles and checks if it is smaller than the sum of their radii, indicating a collision.

Advanced Physics Simulations

Advanced physics simulations add an extra layer of realism to games by incorporating concepts like friction, momentum, and more complex collision responses. These simulations often require a deeper understanding of physics principles and may involve third-party libraries.

Momentum and Impulse

In games where objects collide, momentum plays a key role in determining how they behave after the collision. The concept of momentum can be simulated by applying forces to objects when they collide, based on their mass and velocity.

Friction

Friction affects how objects move across surfaces, slowing them down over time. This can be simulated by reducing an object's velocity over time, proportional to a friction constant.

```python
FRICTION = 0.1

def apply_friction():

if on_ground:

player_vel[0] *= (1 - FRICTION) # Reduce horizontal velocity
```

This code applies friction to slow the player down when they are on the ground.

Rigid Body Dynamics

More advanced simulations involve rigid body dynamics, where objects have mass and interact with one another through forces like collision impulses. For complex simulations like these, you may consider integrating a physics engine like PyMunk, which provides robust tools for simulating realistic physics in games.

Chapter 8: Creating a Simple Game: Pong

Planning the Game

Before starting development on Pong, it's important to understand the mechanics of the game. Pong is one of the simplest arcade games ever created, where two paddles controlled by the players are used to hit a ball back and forth. The objective of the game is to prevent the ball from passing your paddle while trying to score by getting the ball past your opponent's paddle. In our implementation, we will:

- Set up two paddles, one on the left side and one on the right.

- Have a ball that bounces around the screen and interacts with the paddles.

- Allow players to control the paddles using keyboard input.

- Keep score when the ball passes the paddles.

Basic Mechanics Overview

The game consists of a few main elements:

1. **Paddles**: Two rectangular paddles that move up and down.
2. **Ball**: A ball that moves across the screen, bouncing off the paddles and walls.
3. **Score**: A scoring system that tracks points when a player misses the ball.

We will use Pygame's built-in functions for collision detection, rendering shapes, and handling input to simplify the development process.

Planning the Game Environment

The screen will be split into three main areas:

1. The left side of the screen will contain Player 1's paddle.
2. The right side will contain Player 2's paddle.
3. The ball will start from the center of the screen and move toward one of the paddles.

The game will be displayed on a Pygame window with a fixed size, e.g., 800x600 pixels. The ball will move at a constant speed, and the paddles will move vertically based on player input. We will also add boundary conditions to ensure that the paddles don't move off-screen.

Setting Up the Game Environment

Initializing Pygame

To begin, we need to set up the Pygame environment. This includes initializing Pygame, setting up the screen dimensions, and defining the game clock to control the game speed.

```
import pygame

# Initialize Pygame

pygame.init()

# Set up the game window dimensions

screen_width = 800
```

```python
screen_height = 600

screen = pygame.display.set_mode((screen_width, screen_height))

# Set the title of the game window

pygame.display.set_caption('Pong')

# Define game clock

clock = pygame.time.Clock()
```

Defining Colors and Game Variables

We'll define some essential colors for our game, such as white for the paddles and ball and black for the background.

```python
# Colors (RGB)

white = (255, 255, 255)

black = (0, 0, 0)

# Paddle settings

paddle_width = 10

paddle_height = 100

# Ball settings

ball_size = 20
```

Creating Game Objects

We need to represent the paddles and ball as objects in the game. This can be achieved by using simple Pygame Rect objects.

```python
# Paddle positions
```

```python
left_paddle = pygame.Rect(50, (screen_height // 2) - (paddle_height
// 2), paddle_width, paddle_height)

right_paddle = pygame.Rect(screen_width - 60, (screen_height // 2) -
(paddle_height // 2), paddle_width, paddle_height)

# Ball position and movement

ball = pygame.Rect(screen_width // 2, screen_height // 2, ball_size,
ball_size)

ball_dx = 5 # Ball's speed in the x direction

ball_dy = 5 # Ball's speed in the y direction
```

With this, the basic environment setup is done. The next step is implementing the game mechanics.

Implementing Game Mechanics

Ball Movement

The core of Pong is the ball bouncing back and forth between the two paddles. To achieve this, we need to move the ball based on its velocity and check for collisions with the paddles and the screen boundaries.

```python
def move_ball():

global ball_dx, ball_dy

ball.x += ball_dx

ball.y += ball_dy

# Bounce off top and bottom

if ball.top <= 0 or ball.bottom >= screen_height:
```

```python
ball_dy = -ball_dy

# Reset ball if it goes out of bounds

if ball.left <= 0 or ball.right >= screen_width:

ball.x = screen_width // 2

ball.y = screen_height // 2

ball_dx = -ball_dx # Change ball direction
```

Paddle Movement

Player 1 and Player 2 will control the left and right paddles, respectively. We'll use the pygame.key.get_pressed() function to detect keyboard input and move the paddles up and down.

```python
def move_paddles(keys):

# Player 1 (left paddle)

if keys[pygame.K_w] and left_paddle.top > 0:

left_paddle.y -= 5

if keys[pygame.K_s] and left_paddle.bottom < screen_height:

left_paddle.y += 5

# Player 2 (right paddle)

if keys[pygame.K_UP] and right_paddle.top > 0:

right_paddle.y -= 5

if keys[pygame.K_DOWN] and right_paddle.bottom <
screen_height:
```

```
right_paddle.y += 5
```

Paddle and Ball Collision

When the ball reaches the paddles, we need to check for collisions and reverse the ball's direction if a collision occurs.

```python
def check_collision():

global ball_dx

if ball.colliderect(left_paddle) or ball.colliderect(right_paddle):

ball_dx = -ball_dx
```

Adding Sound and Final Touches

Adding Sound Effects

To enhance the game experience, we can add simple sound effects for when the ball bounces off the paddles or walls. Pygame's mixer module makes this straightforward.

```python
# Load sound effects

bounce_sound = pygame.mixer.Sound('bounce.wav')

score_sound = pygame.mixer.Sound('score.wav')

def play_sound(effect):

if effect == 'bounce':

bounce_sound.play()

elif effect == 'score':

score_sound.play()
```

Now, play the sound whenever the ball hits the paddle or a wall.

```python
def check_collision():
    global ball_dx
    if ball.colliderect(left_paddle) or ball.colliderect(right_paddle):
        ball_dx = -ball_dx
        play_sound('bounce')
```

Scoring System

We need to track the score for both players. Each time the ball passes a paddle, the opponent scores a point.

```python
# Initial scores
left_score = 0
right_score = 0

def check_score():
    global left_score, right_score
    if ball.left <= 0:
        right_score += 1
        play_sound('score')
    if ball.right >= screen_width:
        left_score += 1
        play_sound('score')
```

The game now has sound, paddle controls, and a scoring system.

Displaying the Score

We can render the score using Pygame's font module to show the players' current scores.

```
# Initialize font

font = pygame.font.Font(None, 74)

def display_score():

left_text = font.render(str(left_score), True, white)

right_text = font.render(str(right_score), True, white)

screen.blit(left_text, (screen_width // 4, 20))

screen.blit(right_text, (screen_width * 3 // 4, 20))
```

Finally, call this function inside the game loop to continuously update the score on the screen.

With these final touches, the Pong game is complete. All core mechanics, including movement, collisions, scoring, and sound, have been implemented.

Chapter 9: Game Development Techniques

Game State Management

In game development, managing the various states of your game is crucial for creating a seamless and interactive experience. Game states represent different stages or modes within your game, such as the main menu, settings, gameplay, pause screen, and game over screen. Proper game state management allows you to transition smoothly between these modes and maintain organized, maintainable code.

One common approach to managing game states is by implementing a state machine. A state machine keeps track of the current state and defines how the game transitions from one state to another based on events or conditions. In Python and Pygame, you can create a simple state machine using classes or functions to represent each state.

Here's an example using classes:

```python
class GameState:

def __init__(self):

self.state = 'menu'

def switch_state(self, new_state):

self.state = new_state

def update(self):

if self.state == 'menu':

self.menu_update()
```

```python
elif self.state == 'play':

self.play_update()

elif self.state == 'pause':

self.pause_update()

def menu_update(self):

# Handle menu logic

pass

def play_update(self):

# Handle gameplay logic

pass

def pause_update(self):

# Handle pause logic

pass
```

In this example, the GameState class manages different states by switching between methods corresponding to each state. This approach keeps your game loop clean and separates the logic for each state.

Managing game states effectively also involves handling inputs and events specific to each state. For instance, the keys or buttons active during gameplay might differ from those in the main menu. By isolating input handling within each state, you prevent unwanted interactions and improve user experience.

Another important aspect is resource management. Loading and unloading assets like images, sounds, or level data should be handled carefully to optimize performance. When switching states, you might need to free up memory by deleting unnecessary objects or loading new resources required for the next state.

State transitions should be smooth to maintain immersion. This can be achieved by implementing transition effects such as fade-ins, fade-outs, or animations. These effects can enhance the visual appeal and professionalism of your game.

Complex games may require nested states or substates. For example, a pause menu might appear during gameplay, but you still want the background to display the current game screen. In such cases, stacking states or using a stack-based state machine can be effective.

```python
class StateMachine:

def __init__(self):

self.states = []

def push_state(self, state):

self.states.append(state)

def pop_state(self):

self.states.pop()

def current_state(self):

return self.states[-1]
```

This stack-based approach allows you to overlay states and return to previous ones seamlessly.

Testing and debugging become more manageable with proper game state management. Isolating code for each state means you can test them independently, reducing the likelihood of bugs and making them easier to fix.

In summary, game state management is a foundational practice in game development that contributes to clean code architecture and a polished user experience. By thoughtfully designing your state system, you set the stage for a scalable and maintainable game.

Handling Multiple Levels and Scenes

Creating games with multiple levels or scenes adds depth and variety, keeping players engaged and challenged. In Pygame, handling multiple levels involves organizing your game's structure to load different environments, enemies, and objectives seamlessly.

One effective method is to abstract level data from your main codebase. You can store level configurations in external files like JSON, XML, or even custom text files. This approach allows you to design levels without hardcoding them, making your game more flexible and easier to update.

Here's how you might load level data from a JSON file:

```
import json

def load_level(level_number):

with open(f'levels/level_{level_number}.json', 'r') as file:

level_data = json.load(file)

return level_data
```

By loading level data dynamically, you can create a loop that progresses through levels based on player actions. This also simplifies adding new levels—just create a new data file, and your game can load it without additional code changes.

Managing scenes, such as menus, cutscenes, or credits, follows a similar principle. Each scene can be a separate module or class with its own logic for rendering and updating. You can use a scene manager to switch between these scenes:

```python
class SceneManager:

def __init__(self):

self.scenes = {}

self.current_scene = None

def add_scene(self, name, scene):

self.scenes[name] = scene

def switch_to(self, name):

self.current_scene = self.scenes[name]

def update(self):

self.current_scene.update()

def render(self, screen):

self.current_scene.render(screen)
```

This modular design keeps your main game loop clean and delegates responsibility to individual scene classes.

When dealing with multiple levels, consider implementing a level loader that not only reads the level data but also initializes all the necessary game objects like enemies, platforms, and collectibles. This loader can handle positioning, properties, and behaviors defined in your level files.

Transition effects between levels and scenes enhance the player's experience. Simple animations like fades or slides make transitions feel deliberate and polished. Implementing these effects requires careful timing and possibly pausing game logic during the transition.

Memory management is crucial when loading and unloading levels. Ensure that you're properly disposing of objects from previous levels to free up resources. Python's garbage collector handles unreferenced objects, but explicitly deleting large or numerous objects can be beneficial.

Testing each level individually helps identify issues early. Automated tests or debug modes that allow you to jump to specific levels can save time during development.

In multiplayer or networked games, synchronizing levels between clients becomes essential. Make sure your level loading mechanism accounts for network latency and data consistency.

Finally, think about scalability. As your game grows, you might want to include features like a level editor, procedural generation, or downloadable content. Designing your level and scene management with future expansion in mind will save you significant effort down the line.

Saving and Loading Game Data

Implementing a save and load system is vital for enhancing player experience, allowing them to pause and resume gameplay at their convenience. In Pygame, you can achieve this by serializing game state data and writing it to a file, which can later be read to restore the game state.

One common method for saving data is using the JSON format due to its readability and ease of use. Here's a simple example:

```python
import json

def save_game(data, filename='savegame.json'):

with open(filename, 'w') as file:

json.dump(data, file)

def load_game(filename='savegame.json'):

with open(filename, 'r') as file:

data = json.load(file)

return data
```

The data dictionary might contain player stats, inventory, level progress, and settings. Ensure that all the data types within the dictionary are serializable (e.g., numbers, strings, lists, and other dictionaries).

When saving game data, consider what information is essential to recreate the game state accurately. Overwriting previous save files or implementing multiple save slots are design choices that affect how players interact with your game.

For more complex data structures or for added security (to prevent players from easily editing save files), you might use Python's pickle module. However, be cautious with pickle as it can execute arbitrary code during unpickling, posing a security risk if the save file is tampered with.

```python
import pickle

def save_game(data, filename='savegame.dat'):
    with open(filename, 'wb') as file:
        pickle.dump(data, file)

def load_game(filename='savegame.dat'):
    with open(filename, 'rb') as file:
        data = pickle.load(file)
        return data
```

Always validate and sanitize data loaded from external sources to prevent potential exploits.

In addition to manual saving, implementing auto-save features at checkpoints or after significant events can enhance user experience by reducing the loss of progress due to unforeseen circumstances like crashes.

Consider encrypting save files if your game involves sensitive information or to prevent cheating. Lightweight encryption can deter casual tampering.

Settings and preferences are also part of game data that can be saved separately. Storing user settings in a configuration file allows players to retain their preferred control schemes, audio levels, and graphical options between sessions.

Cloud saving is an advanced feature that syncs player progress across devices. While more complex to implement, it significantly enhances accessibility and convenience for players.

Remember to comply with data protection laws and respect user privacy when handling and storing personal data, especially if you're integrating online features.

In testing your save and load system, ensure that all possible game states can be correctly serialized and deserialized. Corrupted save files can lead to crashes or loss of progress, which can be frustrating for players.

In summary, a robust saving and loading mechanism is essential for modern games, contributing to a positive player experience and the overall success of your game.

Optimizing Game Performance

Optimizing your game's performance is crucial to ensure a smooth and enjoyable experience for players. Performance issues can lead to lag, stuttering, or crashes, which detract from gameplay. Here are several strategies to optimize your Pygame project.

Efficient Rendering: Redrawing the entire screen every frame can be resource-intensive. Instead, use dirty rectangles or update only the parts of the screen that have changed.

```
pygame.display.update(dirty_rects)
```

By keeping track of areas that need redrawing, you reduce the workload on the CPU and GPU.

Sprite Groups and Batching: Utilize pygame.sprite.Group to manage and draw multiple sprites efficiently. Grouping sprites allows you to update and draw them with fewer function calls.

```
all_sprites = pygame.sprite.Group()

all_sprites.add(player, enemies, platforms)
```

```
all_sprites.update()

all_sprites.draw(screen)
```

Optimize Collision Detection: Collision checks can be a performance bottleneck, especially with many objects. Use spatial partitioning techniques like quad-trees or grids to limit the number of checks.

Resource Management: Load assets like images and sounds once and reuse them to avoid unnecessary disk I/O and memory usage. Create a resource manager to handle loading and caching of assets.

```
class ResourceManager:

def __init__(self):

self.images = {}

def load_image(self, path):

if path not in self.images:

self.images[path] = pygame.image.load(path).convert_alpha()

return self.images[path]
```

Limit Expensive Operations: Avoid performing heavy computations or loading resources during the game loop. Pre-calculate values and load assets during initialization or in a separate loading screen.

Frame Rate Management: Control the game's frame rate using pygame.time.Clock to ensure consistent timing across different hardware.

```
clock = pygame.time.Clock()

while running:
```

```
# Game loop logic

clock.tick(60) # Limit to 60 FPS
```

Use Profiling Tools: Identify performance hotspots by profiling your code. Python's built-in cProfile module or external tools can help pinpoint inefficient code sections.

Optimize Data Structures: Choose appropriate data structures for your needs. For example, use lists for ordered collections and dictionaries for fast lookups.

Memory Management: Be mindful of memory usage by deleting unused objects and freeing resources. While Python has garbage collection, explicitly managing memory can prevent leaks in complex applications.

Minimize State Changes: When rendering, minimize changes to drawing states like color or blending modes. Batch similar drawing operations together.

Code Optimization:

- Use local variables inside loops to speed up variable access.

- Avoid global variables when possible.

- Simplify mathematical calculations.

Consider Compiling with Cython: For performance-critical sections, consider using Cython to compile Python code into C, offering significant speed improvements.

Threading and Multiprocessing: Offload non-graphical, CPU-intensive tasks to separate threads or processes. Be cautious with threading in Pygame, as it is not thread-safe for rendering operations.

Hardware Acceleration: Enable hardware acceleration if available. Pygame supports OpenGL, which can leverage GPU capabilities for rendering.

Asset Optimization:

- Compress images and sounds without sacrificing quality.

- Use appropriate image formats (e.g., PNG for lossless compression).

- Reduce the resolution of assets where high detail is unnecessary.

Testing on Target Hardware: Test your game on various systems to identify performance issues that may not appear on your development machine.

In conclusion, performance optimization is an ongoing process that requires attention to detail and thorough testing. By implementing these strategies, you enhance the playability and appeal of your game across a wider range of hardware configurations.

Chapter 10: Advanced Pygame Features

Using Pygame's Built-In Functions

Pygame offers a wide range of built-in functions that can help streamline game development. Understanding and leveraging these functions can save time and effort, enabling you to focus more on game design rather than writing low-level code. Some of these built-in functions are used for drawing, event handling, or managing time and resources.

One of the most commonly used functions in Pygame is pygame.draw. This function allows you to draw simple shapes such as rectangles, circles, lines, and polygons. Here is an example of how you can draw a rectangle:

```python
import pygame

pygame.init()

screen = pygame.display.set_mode((400, 300))

# Colors

white = (255, 255, 255)

blue = (0, 0, 255)

# Drawing a blue rectangle

pygame.draw.rect(screen, blue, (100, 100, 60, 60))

pygame.display.flip()

pygame.quit()
```

This code draws a blue rectangle on the screen. The pygame.draw.rect() function takes four arguments: the surface to draw on, the color, and the position and size of the rectangle.

Another essential built-in function is pygame.time.Clock(). This function is crucial for controlling the frame rate of your game, which in turn affects how smoothly your game runs. By setting a frame rate limit, you can ensure that your game performs consistently across different systems.

clock = pygame.time.Clock()

Set the frame rate

frame_rate = 60

In the game loop

clock.tick(frame_rate)

In the example above, the tick() method is used to limit the game loop to 60 frames per second. Without this, the game may run too fast, depending on the speed of the system running it.

Event handling is another vital part of Pygame's functionality. The pygame.event.get() function is used to capture all the events happening in your game, such as keyboard or mouse input. Here's an example of handling a keypress event:

for event in pygame.event.get():

if event.type == pygame.QUIT:

running = False

elif event.type == pygame.KEYDOWN:

```
if event.key == pygame.K_SPACE:
```

```
print("Spacebar pressed")
```

This snippet checks for events in the game loop. If the player presses the spacebar, the program prints "Spacebar pressed". Pygame has built-in constants for all common keys, which can make key handling straightforward.

Another useful set of built-in functions are related to sound. Using the pygame.mixer module, you can easily load and play sounds in your game. Here's how you can load and play a sound effect:

```
pygame.mixer.init()
```

```
sound = pygame.mixer.Sound("sound_effect.wav")
```

```
sound.play()
```

The pygame.mixer.Sound function loads a sound file, and the play() method starts playing it. This simple interface makes it easy to add sound effects to your game.

Finally, Pygame offers numerous utility functions for handling surfaces, managing the display, and more. For instance, pygame.Surface() allows you to create surfaces that can be drawn onto before displaying them on the main screen.

```
surface = pygame.Surface((100, 100))
```

```
surface.fill((255, 0, 0))
```

```
screen.blit(surface, (50, 50))
```
```
pygame.display.flip()
```

In this code, we create a red 100x100 surface, fill it with red, and then blit it to the main display at position (50, 50). Blitting is the process of copying one image surface onto another.

Overall, Pygame's built-in functions are indispensable for rapid game development. Mastering them will enable you to build games more efficiently while maintaining control over the game's essential elements.

Extending Pygame with External Libraries

While Pygame provides many built-in functions, sometimes you may need to extend its capabilities using external libraries. Python has a rich ecosystem of libraries, many of which can be integrated with Pygame to add features such as advanced graphics, networking, or physics simulations.

One common use case for extending Pygame is for physics simulations. Although Pygame offers basic collision detection and response, libraries like Pymunk or Box2D can provide more advanced physics simulations. Pymunk, for example, is a 2D physics engine that integrates well with Pygame.

Here's an example of using Pymunk with Pygame:

```python
import pygame

import pymunk

def create_circle(space, pos):

body = pymunk.Body(1, pymunk.inf)

body.position = pos

shape = pymunk.Circle(body, 25)
```

```python
space.add(body, shape)

return shape

# Initialize Pygame and Pymunk

pygame.init()

screen = pygame.display.set_mode((600, 400))

clock = pygame.time.Clock()

space = pymunk.Space()

space.gravity = (0, 900)

# Create a ball

ball = create_circle(space, (300, 50))

# Main loop

running = True

while running:

    for event in pygame.event.get():

        if event.type == pygame.QUIT:

            running = False

    # Update physics

    space.step(1/60.0)

    # Clear screen

    screen.fill((255, 255, 255))
```

```python
# Draw the ball

pygame.draw.circle(screen, (0, 0, 255), (int(ball.body.position.x), int(ball.body.position.y)), 25)

pygame.display.flip()

clock.tick(60)

pygame.quit()
```

In this code, we use Pymunk to handle the physics of a falling ball. The ball is affected by gravity, and Pymunk takes care of the simulation. Integrating a library like Pymunk allows for more realistic game physics without having to implement them from scratch.

Another useful extension is for networking. Pygame doesn't have built-in networking support, but libraries like socket or Twisted can help you build multiplayer games. For example, you can use Python's socket library to set up a basic client-server architecture for a multiplayer game.

```python
import socket

# Server

server_socket = socket.socket(socket.AF_INET, socket.SOCK_STREAM)

server_socket.bind(('localhost', 5555))

server_socket.listen(2)

client_socket, addr = server_socket.accept()

print(f"Connected by {addr}")

# Client
```

```
client_socket = socket.socket(socket.AF_INET, socket.SOCK_STREAM)

client_socket.connect(('localhost', 5555))

client_socket.sendall(b"Hello, Server")
```

This code shows the basic setup of a server and client connection. Once the connection is established, the client can send data to the server. Although simplistic, this forms the foundation of any multiplayer networking feature.

For advanced graphics, libraries like PyOpenGL can be used alongside Pygame to handle more complex 3D rendering. Pygame itself is primarily a 2D game engine, but PyOpenGL can help render 3D objects within a Pygame window.

```
from OpenGL.GL import *

from OpenGL.GLUT import *

from OpenGL.GLU import *

# Example of initializing PyOpenGL within a Pygame window
```

This can be especially useful for developers looking to experiment with 3D graphics while still utilizing Pygame's input handling and event systems.

In summary, extending Pygame with external libraries allows you to add more sophisticated features to your game, from physics simulations to multiplayer networking and advanced graphics. These external libraries can enhance your game's performance and capabilities, providing a richer experience for the player.

Networking and Multiplayer Games

Creating multiplayer games can significantly enhance the experience by allowing players to interact with one another. Pygame does not natively support networking, but Python's socket library and other external libraries can be used to implement multiplayer functionality.

To start, let's discuss the basics of using the socket library to create a simple client-server architecture. In multiplayer games, the server handles the game state, while clients send player inputs and receive updates from the server.

Here's an example of setting up a basic server using socket:

```python
import socket

server_socket = socket.socket(socket.AF_INET, socket.SOCK_STREAM)

server_socket.bind(('localhost', 5555))

server_socket.listen(2)

print("Server started, waiting for players...")

while True:

client_socket, addr = server_socket.accept()

print(f"Player connected from {addr}")
```

This code sets up a simple server that listens for incoming connections. When a player connects, the server accepts the connection and prints a message indicating that a player has joined.

On the client side, you can create a connection to the server like this:

```python
import socket
```

```
client_socket                =                socket.socket(socket.AF_INET,
socket.SOCK_STREAM)
```

```
client_socket.connect(('localhost', 5555))
```

```
print("Connected to the server!")
```

Once the connection is established, data can be exchanged between the server and the clients. For instance, you can send player positions and other game state data from the clients to the server.

To make the communication between the server and clients more robust, you can implement a simple protocol for handling different game events. For example, you could define message types like "MOVE" for player movement or "SCORE" for sending score updates. Here's an example of how you might implement this:

```python
# Server-side handling of messages

def handle_client(client_socket):

while True:

msg = client_socket.recv(1024).decode('utf-8')

if msg.startswith("MOVE"):

# Process player movement

pass

elif msg.startswith("SCORE"):

# Update the score
pass
```

In this case, the server processes incoming messages based on their type. The recv() function receives data from the client, and the server can then handle it appropriately.

To support multiple players, you can use threading to handle each client in its own thread. Python's threading module can help here:

import threading

def handle_client(client_socket):

Code to handle client interaction

pass

while True:

client_socket, addr = server_socket.accept()

thread = threading.Thread(target=handle_client, args=(client_socket,))

thread.start()

With this setup, the server can handle multiple clients simultaneously by spawning a new thread for each connection. This allows for real-time multiplayer interaction, where each client sends input to the server and receives updates on the game state.

Another consideration for multiplayer games is synchronization. The server must ensure that all clients have an up-to-date view of the game state. This can be achieved by broadcasting updates to all clients whenever a change occurs. For example:

def broadcast(message, clients):

for client in clients:

```
client.sendall(message.encode('utf-8'))
```

In this code, the broadcast() function sends a message to all connected clients, ensuring that everyone is aware of the latest game state.

Networking also introduces latency, which can affect gameplay. To minimize the impact of latency, you can implement techniques like client-side prediction and server reconciliation. Client-side prediction allows the player's actions to be processed immediately on the client side, while the server verifies and corrects the game state if necessary.

For more complex multiplayer games, you may want to consider using a higher-level networking library like Twisted or ZeroMQ. These libraries provide more advanced features, such as asynchronous networking and message queuing, which can simplify the development of large-scale multiplayer games.

In conclusion, adding networking capabilities to your Pygame game allows for a richer, multiplayer experience. By using Python's socket library or other networking tools, you can create both simple and complex multiplayer architectures, enabling players to interact and compete in real time.

Debugging and Testing Your Game

Debugging and testing are essential aspects of game development, ensuring that your game runs smoothly and without errors. Pygame provides several tools and techniques for identifying and fixing bugs during development.

One of the simplest yet most effective debugging techniques is logging. By logging key information during your game's runtime, you can track the flow of execution and identify when something goes wrong. Python's built-in logging module can be used for this purpose:

```
import logging

logging.basicConfig(level=logging.DEBUG)

logging.debug('This is a debug message')

logging.info('This is an info message')

logging.warning('This is a warning message')
```

With logging in place, you can insert log statements throughout your code to monitor variables, function calls, and the general flow of your game. This makes it easier to pinpoint where errors occur and understand the conditions leading to them.

Another important technique is exception handling. By using try-except blocks, you can catch errors before they cause your game to crash. Here's an example:

```
try:

# Code that might throw an exception

player.move()

except Exception as e:

logging.error(f"An error occurred: {e}")
```

In this code, if an error occurs in the player.move() function, it will be caught, and an error message will be logged. This prevents the game from crashing and allows you to handle the error more gracefully.

Testing is another critical part of game development. Unit testing can be used to verify the functionality of individual components of your game. Python's unittest module is a great tool for writing tests. Here's an example of a simple unit test:

```python
import unittest

from game import Player

class TestPlayer(unittest.TestCase):

def test_player_move(self):

player = Player()

player.move(10)

self.assertEqual(player.position, 10)
```

In this test, we check whether the player's position updates correctly after calling the move() function. By writing unit tests for your game's components, you can ensure that each part of your game behaves as expected.

Pygame also offers tools for measuring the performance of your game. You can use the pygame.time.get_ticks() function to track how long different parts of your code take to execute. This can help you identify performance bottlenecks and optimize your game accordingly.

```python
start_time = pygame.time.get_ticks()

# Code you want to measure

player.move()

end_time = pygame.time.get_ticks()

execution_time = end_time - start_time

print(f"Execution time: {execution_time} ms")
```

If your game is running slower than expected, you can use this technique to find out which parts of your code are taking the longest to execute and focus your optimization efforts there.

Another useful tool for debugging in Pygame is the pygame.draw.rect() function, which can be used to visualize collision boxes and other invisible elements in your game. For example, if your game uses bounding boxes for collision detection, you can draw them on the screen to ensure they are correctly positioned:

pygame.draw.rect(screen, (255, 0, 0), player.bounding_box, 2)

This draws a red rectangle around the player's bounding box, making it easier to see whether the collisions are being detected correctly.

When testing your game, it's important to cover all possible scenarios, including edge cases and uncommon inputs. For instance, you should test what happens if the player tries to move outside the bounds of the screen, or if two objects collide at an unexpected angle. By thoroughly testing your game, you can ensure that it handles all situations gracefully.

Finally, user feedback is a valuable part of the debugging and testing process. Once you've tested your game internally, you can release it to a small group of beta testers. These testers can provide feedback on bugs, performance issues, and overall gameplay experience. Their feedback can help you identify problems that you might not have noticed during development.

In conclusion, debugging and testing are critical for delivering a polished, bug-free game. By using logging, exception handling, unit tests, and performance profiling, you can identify and fix issues before they affect your players. Combined with user feedback, these techniques will help you create a more stable and enjoyable game.

Chapter 11: Developing a Platformer Game

Game Design and Planning

Designing a platformer game involves several steps, from outlining the game's core mechanics to deciding on the art style and sound design. Before diving into coding, it's essential to have a clear plan for how the game will work and feel. The first step in designing a platformer is deciding on the key mechanics such as jumping, running, and interacting with the environment. These mechanics form the backbone of your game and will influence every other design decision you make.

Another crucial aspect of game design is setting the theme. Will your platformer be a traditional side-scroller, or will it have vertical elements? Perhaps it's a puzzle platformer where players must solve environmental puzzles to progress. Establishing the genre and style early on helps guide the development process and ensures consistency throughout the game.

Next, it's important to sketch out level designs. Each level should introduce new challenges or mechanics to keep players engaged. You may want to start simple, gradually increasing the difficulty as the player advances. Think about pacing—how often will players face difficult challenges, and how much downtime will they have to explore or recover?

Once the basic mechanics and level designs are set, think about the narrative. While not all platformers require a story, a simple narrative can give players a sense of purpose and direction. Whether it's rescuing a character, collecting items, or defeating enemies, a clear goal will help drive the player's actions.

Finally, create a technical design document (TDD). This document outlines the technical specifications, including the game's architecture, file formats, physics engine, and third-party libraries you'll be using. Having a well-documented TDD will make the development process smoother and help when collaborating with other developers or artists.

Building the Game World

Building a platformer's game world involves creating the physical environment in which the player will navigate. The core of any platformer is its level layout, which includes platforms, obstacles, enemies, and collectables. In Pygame, building the world begins with creating the basic level structure.

The first step is creating tiles that represent the floor, walls, and platforms. A tile-based approach makes it easier to construct and manage the game world. For instance, you can use a simple 2D array to define the level's layout, where each number corresponds to a specific tile type:

level = [

[1, 1, 1, 1, 1, 1, 1, 1, 1],

[1, 0, 0, 0, 0, 0, 0, 0, 1],

[1, 0, 1, 1, 1, 0, 1, 0, 1],

[1, 0, 1, 0, 1, 0, 1, 0, 1],

[1, 0, 0, 0, 0, 0, 0, 0, 1],

[1, 1, 1, 1, 1, 1, 1, 1, 1]

]

In this example, 1 represents solid tiles, and 0 represents empty space. You can then render these tiles to the screen using Pygame's drawing functions, or better yet, load tile images for a more visually appealing world.

You should also focus on parallax scrolling, which adds depth to the game world. Parallax scrolling involves having multiple background layers that move at different speeds, giving the illusion of depth. Implementing parallax scrolling can be done by adjusting the speed at which each background layer moves relative to the player's movement speed.

In terms of collision detection, you'll need to define which tiles or objects in the world are solid so that the player can't pass through them. Pygame's colliderect() function can be used to handle collisions between the player and the environment.

Finally, designing a world involves deciding on the visual style and aesthetic. Will your game have pixel art, or will it be more cartoonish or realistic? The art style plays a significant role in setting the game's tone and atmosphere. Along with visuals, don't forget to place environmental hazards, such as spikes, pits, or moving platforms, which can add challenge and excitement to the gameplay.

Character Controls and Enemy AI

Character controls in a platformer game are a fundamental aspect that can make or break the player's experience. The character's movement should feel smooth and responsive, with precise control over jumping, running, and stopping. In Pygame, controlling the character involves handling input events from the keyboard or gamepad.

For basic movement, you can track the player's position and velocity, updating them each frame based on input. A typical implementation looks like this:

```
player_velocity_x = 0

player_velocity_y = 0

gravity = 0.5

if keys[K_LEFT]:

player_velocity_x = -5

if keys[K_RIGHT]:

player_velocity_x = 5

if not (keys[K_LEFT] or keys[K_RIGHT]):

player_velocity_x = 0

player_velocity_y += gravity # Gravity effect

player_x += player_velocity_x

player_y += player_velocity_y
```

In this snippet, the player moves left or right based on key input, and gravity is applied to simulate falling. Jumping can be implemented by checking if the player is on the ground before allowing them to jump:

```
if is_on_ground and keys[K_SPACE]:

player_velocity_y = -10
```

Once character movement is smooth, you can turn your attention to enemy AI. Platformer enemies often have simple behavior patterns, such as moving back and forth on a platform or chasing the player when they come within a certain range.

For patrolling enemies, you can alternate the enemy's movement direction when they reach the edge of a platform:

```
enemy_direction = 1

enemy_velocity_x = 2

if enemy_hits_wall():

enemy_direction *= -1

enemy_x += enemy_velocity_x * enemy_direction
```

For more complex AI, such as chasing the player, you can check the player's position relative to the enemy and adjust the enemy's movement accordingly. For example, if the player is to the right of the enemy, the enemy will move to the right:

```
if player_x > enemy_x:

enemy_velocity_x = 2

else:

enemy_velocity_x = -2
```

Implementing different types of enemies, each with unique behaviors, adds variety and challenge to the game. Some enemies may shoot projectiles, others may fly, and some may follow predefined paths. Consider giving each enemy type distinct characteristics that force the player to adjust their approach.

Level Design and Progression

Level design in platformer games plays a crucial role in keeping the player engaged and challenged. A well-designed level introduces new mechanics and obstacles at a steady pace while allowing the player to master them through practice. Early levels should focus on teaching the player the core mechanics, such as running, jumping, and basic enemy interaction, before gradually increasing the complexity.

One approach to level design is to build levels around specific challenges. For example, one level could focus on tricky platforming sections with moving platforms, while another could center around combat with enemies. Mixing these elements ensures that the game doesn't feel repetitive.

Progression is another key aspect of level design. As the player advances, they should feel a sense of accomplishment and progression. This can be achieved by gradually introducing new gameplay mechanics, such as power-ups, new enemy types, or more complex environmental hazards.

Additionally, creating hidden areas or secret paths encourages players to explore the environment. Offering rewards, such as extra lives or power-ups, for finding these secrets adds an extra layer of depth to the game.

To maintain engagement, it's important to balance the difficulty curve. If the game becomes too difficult too quickly, players may become frustrated, while a game that is too easy may feel boring. Playtesting is crucial to ensure that the difficulty increases at a manageable rate, and that each level feels fair but challenging.

Finally, consider how the levels tie together to create a cohesive experience. Will there be a central hub world that connects different levels, or will the game progress linearly from one level to the next? Will players have the ability to revisit completed levels to find secrets or improve their score? All of these decisions contribute to the overall structure and flow of the game, impacting how players experience progression throughout the platformer.

Chapter 12: Publishing and Beyond

Preparing Your Game for Release

Releasing a game is a critical step in the game development process. It's not just about having a finished product; it's about ensuring that your game is polished, bug-free, and ready for public consumption. Here are key steps to take when preparing your game for release:

First, ensure that all core game mechanics are functioning as intended. Thoroughly test each level, interaction, and feature in your game. Make sure to involve different users, ideally from various backgrounds and skill levels, to perform beta testing. This will provide feedback on any overlooked bugs or confusing gameplay elements.

In terms of performance optimization, you need to ensure that the game runs smoothly across different hardware configurations. Optimize assets such as textures, audio, and sprites to reduce load times and prevent lag. The use of tools like **cProfile** for Python can help you identify bottlenecks in your game's code.

Next, address any accessibility concerns. Adding features such as customizable controls, scalable fonts, and subtitles can make your game more accessible to a broader audience. Consider providing options to adjust difficulty levels, color-blind modes, and keyboard remapping to ensure inclusivity.

Another important step is to implement a save and load system if your game requires it. Ensure that your players can save their progress seamlessly. Make sure to test your save system thoroughly to avoid issues like corrupt save files, which can frustrate users.

Once the game is polished, it's time to build a release version. Use tools like **PyInstaller** or **cx_Freeze** to package your Python-based game into a standalone executable file. These tools will bundle Python with your game, allowing users to run it without needing a separate Python installation. It's also important to strip out any debug logs and unused code from the final build to reduce its size and improve performance.

Additionally, consider adding anti-piracy measures to your game. While it's impossible to completely eliminate piracy, basic steps such as implementing serial keys, user verification, or restricting access to certain features for non-authenticated users can help reduce illegal distribution.

To make your game stand out visually, include a high-quality splash screen and main menu. A professional and user-friendly interface helps establish a positive first impression. Your game's title screen, buttons, and overall UI should align with the style and mood of your game.

When you're ready to release, create multiple builds targeting different platforms. For example, if you're releasing on Windows, Mac, and Linux, ensure that your game runs seamlessly on each of these operating systems. It may also be worthwhile to test your game on different screen resolutions and aspect ratios to ensure a consistent user experience.

In summary, preparing your game for release involves thorough testing, optimizing performance, packaging the game for easy distribution, and ensuring a smooth and polished player experience. These steps are essential to make a positive impact when your game finally hits the market.

Distribution Platforms and Options

Once your game is ready for release, choosing the right distribution platform is essential to reach your target audience. Today, there are many platforms available, each with its own benefits and drawbacks.

The decision will depend largely on your goals, the type of game you've developed, and the platform you've built it for.

One of the most popular platforms for distributing indie games is **Steam**. Steam provides access to a huge user base, but it also requires developers to pay a fee to get their game listed. Steam's platform allows you to sell your game, provide updates, and interact with your player base. Steam Direct is their platform for indie developers, offering an easy-to-follow process to get your game listed.

If you've developed a game for mobile platforms, **Google Play** and the **Apple App Store** are obvious choices. These platforms have a straightforward submission process, although they do require your game to meet certain technical and content standards. Keep in mind that both platforms take a percentage of your sales—30% on average.

For indie developers looking for a more community-driven approach, **itch.io** is a great option. This platform allows for flexible pricing models, including pay-what-you-want and free downloads. Itch.io is also known for its indie-friendly approach, providing a platform where smaller developers can share their games with like-minded individuals.

Another rising platform is the **Epic Games Store**, which provides developers with a larger percentage of revenue (88%) compared to Steam's 70%. However, the Epic Games Store has a more selective process and might not accept every game submitted to its platform.

If you're developing for consoles, getting your game on **PlayStation Network**, **Xbox Live**, or **Nintendo eShop** requires more work. These platforms tend to have stricter submission guidelines and may require you to work with an approved publisher. However, the visibility and credibility of having your game available on consoles can outweigh these hurdles.

For those interested in the open-source community, distributing your game via **GitHub** or similar platforms allows you to share your source code with other developers and enthusiasts. While this isn't a direct revenue-generating option, it can help you build a portfolio, gain feedback, and grow a community around your game.

Lastly, don't forget about physical distribution, although this has become less common with the rise of digital downloads. If you're targeting a niche audience, creating a limited physical release of your game, including physical discs, manuals, or collectible items, can help build hype and generate sales.

Choosing the right distribution platform is a critical decision that can influence the success of your game. Each platform has its own pros and cons, and you may want to explore multiple avenues to maximize your game's reach.

Marketing Your Game

Marketing is a crucial step in ensuring the success of your game. Without a solid marketing plan, even the best game can go unnoticed in the crowded marketplace. The following strategies will help you effectively promote your game and reach potential players.

Start by identifying your target audience. Knowing who will most likely play your game helps guide all of your marketing efforts. You can define your audience by genre preference, age group, platform (PC, console, or mobile), and region. Understanding their preferences will help you craft your messaging, choose the right channels, and maximize the impact of your promotional efforts.

Next, create a **game trailer** that highlights your game's best features. A trailer serves as a visual and emotional hook for potential players. It should showcase gameplay, story elements, and unique mechanics that set your game apart from others. Keep it short—around 1-2 minutes—and make sure it leaves the viewer wanting more.

Social media is another powerful tool for promoting your game. Platforms like **Twitter**, **Instagram**, and **TikTok** are great for sharing game updates, teasers, and behind-the-scenes content. Consistent posting builds excitement and maintains interest leading up to your game's release. Engaging directly with your audience by responding to comments, creating polls, and sharing user-generated content can foster a loyal community around your game.

Launching a **website** dedicated to your game can serve as the central hub for all information related to it. On your website, you can provide updates, host your game trailer, and include links to purchase or download your game. It's also a good place to collect email addresses for future marketing campaigns.

Another effective way to promote your game is by collaborating with **streamers and YouTubers**. Reaching out to influencers in the gaming space and providing them with early access to your game can generate buzz. Their reviews, live streams, and Let's Play videos can expose your game to large audiences who may not have otherwise heard of it.

Consider creating a **press kit** for your game. A press kit typically includes high-quality images, logos, a short game description, and any relevant information about the development process. Having these materials available makes it easier for journalists, bloggers, and influencers to cover your game in their articles or videos.

If you have the budget, running **targeted ads** on platforms like **Facebook**, **Google**, or **Reddit** can help boost visibility. You can set specific demographic filters to reach users most likely to be interested in your game. Even with a small budget, targeted ads can help generate attention from the right audience.

Finally, attending **gaming conventions** and **expos** like PAX, GDC, or smaller local events can provide a great opportunity to showcase your game to both players and industry professionals. If attending in person isn't feasible, consider submitting your game to online game festivals or competitions, where it can gain exposure through digital showcases.

Building anticipation and excitement for your game before its release is key to generating sales and creating a dedicated fan base. A well-executed marketing strategy is crucial for standing out in today's competitive game development landscape.

Learning Resources and Community Involvement

Game development is a constantly evolving field, and it's important to stay connected with the community and keep learning new skills. Whether you're an indie developer or part of a larger team, continued learning and community involvement can help you stay ahead of trends, discover new tools, and refine your craft.

One of the best ways to improve your skills is by participating in **game jams**. These events, which often last between 24 and 72 hours, challenge developers to create a game based on a specific theme or set of constraints. Game jams provide a great opportunity to experiment with new ideas, learn from others, and get feedback on your work. Popular platforms for game jams include **Ludum Dare** and **Global Game Jam**.

In addition to game jams, online **tutorials** and **courses** are valuable resources for learning new techniques. Websites like **Udemy**, **Coursera**, and **YouTube** host a wide variety of tutorials that cater to different skill levels and topics. Whether you're looking to improve your programming, art, or design skills, these platforms offer a wealth of information at your fingertips.

Open-source communities, such as those on **GitHub**, provide another avenue for learning. By contributing to open-source projects, you can see how other developers structure their games, handle problems, and optimize code. You can also share your own projects, gather feedback, and get involved in collaborative development efforts.

Getting involved with online **forums** and **discussion groups** is another way to stay connected. Communities like **Reddit's game development forums**, **TIGSource**, and **Discord** servers dedicated to game development offer spaces where developers can ask questions, share knowledge, and provide feedback to one another. Engaging in these communities not only helps you learn, but it also provides networking opportunities that can open doors to collaboration and job opportunities.

Many developers also choose to attend **conferences and workshops**. Events like the **Game Developers Conference (GDC)**, **E3**, and **PAX** are great places to learn from experts, see the latest industry trends, and meet other developers. These events often feature workshops, panels, and presentations on everything from programming techniques to game design theory.

Finally, don't overlook the value of **reading**. There are countless books on game design, development, and psychology that can help you deepen your understanding of the craft. Books like **"The Art of Game Design" by Jesse Schell** or **"Game Programming Patterns" by Robert Nystrom** are considered classics in the field and can provide you with a strong foundation.

Being a part of the game development community and continuously learning from others will keep you motivated and help you grow as a developer.

Chapter 13: Case Studies and Real-World Examples

Successful Games Made with Python and Pygame

Python and Pygame have been instrumental in creating a variety of successful games, from simple 2D platformers to complex simulations. One such example is *Dangerous Dave*, a 2D platformer that was initially created in assembly language but later ported to Python using Pygame. The game demonstrates how Pygame's simplicity can be used to recreate classic gameplay experiences with modern code.

Another notable project is *Frets on Fire*, a popular rhythm-based game that allows players to simulate playing guitar on their keyboards. Written entirely in Python and using Pygame, this game gained a large community following and demonstrated how Python can be used to create engaging and entertaining gameplay. It also featured user-generated content, allowing players to add their own songs, which expanded its replayability significantly.

Games like *PyWeek* showcase an entire competition based on creating games using Python and Pygame in just one week. These competitions are a great platform for both beginners and experienced developers to test their skills. Games created in PyWeek often showcase the wide range of genres that Pygame supports, from puzzle games to real-time strategy.

The success of games like *RetroPie* is another example of Python's utility in the gaming world. Though RetroPie is primarily used for emulation, it includes several Python-based games and utilities, demonstrating how Python and Pygame are flexible enough to be incorporated into broader gaming systems.

A successful multiplayer game written with Pygame is *Salvage Trader*. This game includes space trading and exploration mechanics and was created as an open-source project. It highlights how Pygame can be extended to create multiplayer experiences, and the importance of networking libraries that integrate with Pygame.

Beyond complete games, Python and Pygame have been instrumental in the development of game prototypes and proof-of-concept projects. For instance, several indie developers have used Pygame to test out mechanics and ideas before fully fleshing them out in other engines.

Some games developed with Pygame were later ported to larger game engines, showing that Pygame can be a stepping stone for developers looking to break into more complex game development. Pygame's relative simplicity makes it a perfect environment for iterating on game mechanics without getting bogged down in technical complexity.

Developers who have built successful games with Pygame often cite its ease of use and integration with Python as key benefits. The ability to quickly write and iterate on code allows for a more rapid development process, and Pygame's strong community support ensures that developers can find help when they need it.

One interesting aspect of Pygame's role in game development is the number of educational games and projects developed for learning purposes. Many schools and universities have adopted Pygame for teaching game development and programming concepts, leading to the creation of games that not only entertain but also educate.

The success of games like *Vikings Village*, a multiplayer game written in Python, further proves that Pygame is more than capable of handling more complex game genres. In this game, players can fight each other in an arena, using simple but addictive mechanics to keep them engaged.

In conclusion, Pygame has enabled the creation of a wide variety of successful games. Its ease of use, community support, and adaptability to different gaming genres make it a fantastic tool for both hobbyists and professional developers alike.

Interviews with Game Developers

One of the most compelling ways to learn about game development is to hear directly from developers who have successfully created and released games using Python and Pygame. These developers often provide valuable insights into the challenges they faced, the tools they used, and how they overcame various obstacles.

For example, in an interview with the developer of *Frets on Fire*, they discussed how Pygame allowed them to focus on gameplay mechanics rather than the intricacies of a more complex game engine. The developer explained that Pygame's simplicity enabled rapid prototyping and allowed for creative flexibility. This ability to quickly iterate on ideas was a crucial factor in the game's success.

Another developer, who created *Salvage Trader*, spoke about the challenges of implementing multiplayer functionality in Pygame. They explained how they used external libraries to handle networking, which worked seamlessly with Pygame's event-driven structure. The developer emphasized that while Pygame isn't designed specifically for multiplayer games, its flexibility allowed them to adapt it for their needs.

In an interview with a developer from the *PyWeek* competition, they shared how the tight deadline pushed them to focus on essential game mechanics and forgo unnecessary complexity. Pygame's straightforward approach to handling graphics, sound, and input was vital in helping them meet the competition's constraints. They credited the Pygame community for offering tips and advice that saved time during development.

Another indie developer discussed the transition from using Pygame to larger game engines. They started their game project in Pygame to prototype mechanics and, once they were satisfied with the core gameplay, they ported the game to Unity. The developer highlighted Pygame's role in helping them quickly test ideas without having to deal with more complicated workflows.

Educational game developers have also praised Pygame for its versatility. One developer working on a game to teach basic math concepts shared how Pygame's straightforward programming model made it possible to focus on educational content rather than technical difficulties. The ease of use allowed them to involve non-technical team members in the development process, which led to more effective collaboration.

Developers of arcade-style games, like the team behind *Vikings Village*, discussed how Pygame allowed them to focus on achieving smooth gameplay and responsiveness. They found that Pygame's performance was adequate for their needs and allowed them to build a fun, fast-paced game without needing to optimize extensively.

A recurring theme in these interviews is that Pygame's simplicity is one of its greatest strengths. While it may not be as feature-rich as larger engines, it allows developers to focus on what matters most: the game itself. Whether working on educational games, arcade titles, or multiplayer experiences, developers consistently praise Pygame for getting out of their way and letting them code.

Challenges and Solutions in Game

Development

Game development is full of challenges, and those using Python and Pygame face their own unique set of obstacles. One common issue is performance, as Python isn't as fast as compiled languages like C++ or C#. While Pygame provides an easy-to-use framework, optimizing performance for more complex games can be tricky.

One solution to performance bottlenecks in Pygame is to limit the number of sprites or objects being updated per frame. Developers have found that reducing the number of simultaneous updates can significantly improve frame rates. Another approach is to use dirty sprites, which only redraw parts of the screen that have changed, minimizing the computational load.

Another challenge developers face is managing game state across multiple scenes or levels. Pygame doesn't have built-in scene management, so developers often create their own systems. A common solution is to design a state machine, where each scene is represented as a state, and transitioning between states occurs through a central manager.

Handling complex input systems, such as managing keyboard, mouse, and joystick inputs simultaneously, can also be daunting. Developers have found that creating a custom input handler that maps different input types to game actions is a practical approach. This method ensures that the same game logic can handle all types of inputs, making the game more versatile.

Collision detection is another common issue, especially in platformers and physics-heavy games. Pygame provides basic collision detection methods, but they can become slow when dealing with large numbers of objects. To overcome this, developers use spatial partitioning techniques, such as quadtrees, to reduce the number of collision checks needed per frame.

Audio handling in Pygame can also pose difficulties. The Pygame mixer module is powerful, but it doesn't natively support streaming large audio files. Developers have found workarounds by using external libraries for audio streaming or by breaking larger files into smaller, manageable chunks.

Developers working on multiplayer games with Pygame face unique challenges, as Pygame wasn't designed with networking in mind. However, many have successfully integrated networking libraries like *Twisted* or *PySocket* to handle multiplayer aspects. The key is creating a reliable system for synchronizing game states between different players over a network.

A common issue in 2D games is managing different screen resolutions. Pygame doesn't have automatic scaling, so developers need to manually adjust graphics for different screen sizes. One solution is to design games at a base resolution and scale all assets dynamically depending on the player's screen size.

Memory management is another critical area where developers can face challenges, particularly when dealing with large games. Loading and unloading resources like images, sounds, and levels dynamically, rather than all at once, can help optimize memory usage.

Future Trends in Python Game Development

The future of Python and Pygame in game development is bright, with several exciting trends on the horizon. One trend is the increasing use of Python for game prototyping, even in teams that eventually switch to more complex engines. The simplicity and speed of development in

Python make it an attractive option for quickly testing game mechanics and ideas.

Another trend is the integration of machine learning and artificial intelligence in games. Python's dominance in the AI and data science fields makes it a natural choice for developers looking to incorporate intelligent behavior into their games. Libraries like TensorFlow and PyTorch, combined with Pygame, allow developers to experiment with AI-driven gameplay, such as creating adaptive enemies or procedural level generation.

With the growing interest in virtual and augmented reality, developers are starting to explore how Python can be used in these new areas. While Pygame itself doesn't support VR or AR, external libraries and Python's ability to interface with hardware make it possible to use Python in developing experimental VR and AR prototypes.

Cross-platform development is another exciting trend. Tools like *Kivy* allow Python developers to create games that run on multiple platforms, including mobile devices. Combining these tools with Pygame allows developers to reach a broader audience without having to learn entirely new programming languages or frameworks.

The open-source nature of Pygame is also paving the way for more community-driven improvements. As more developers contribute to the Pygame ecosystem, new features and optimizations are added, making it a more robust tool for game development. Community-created libraries and plugins are becoming more common, allowing developers to extend Pygame's functionality in ways that suit their specific projects.

Finally, the rise of indie game development has been a significant factor in Python and Pygame's popularity. Many indie developers are looking for lightweight, easy-to-learn frameworks that allow them to create games without a steep learning curve. Pygame fits this niche perfectly, and its community continues to grow as more developers turn to Python for game development.

The future of Python in game development may also involve tighter integration with web technologies. Frameworks like *Pyodide* allow Python to run in the browser, potentially opening up new possibilities for browser-based games written in Python.

Overall, Python and Pygame are well-positioned to continue thriving in the game development world, particularly for indie developers, educators, and those interested in rapid prototyping. The community-driven nature of Pygame and the broader Python ecosystem ensures that developers will continue to innovate and push the boundaries of what can be achieved with these tools.

Chapter 14: Appendices

Glossary of Pygame & Python Terms

Understanding the key terms used in Pygame and Python is essential for effective game development. Below is a glossary of important terms that you may encounter while working with Pygame and Python:

Pygame: A set of Python modules designed for writing video games. Pygame includes computer graphics and sound libraries designed to be used with the Python programming language.

Surface: A fundamental object in Pygame that represents any 2D image or shape. It is where all the drawing happens. Surfaces can be manipulated to display various graphical elements such as shapes, text, and sprites.

Sprite: A 2D image or animation that is integrated into a larger scene. Sprites can be characters, objects, or any element that you want to manipulate independently within a game.

Rect (Rectangle): A Pygame object used to define the position and size of a surface. Rects are used extensively in collision detection and for positioning graphical objects.

Game Loop: The core structure of a game that continues running until the game is closed. In Pygame, this loop handles events, updates game logic, and renders graphics on the screen.

Event Handling: Pygame uses an event queue to manage interactions from the player, such as keyboard and mouse input. The event queue is polled continuously in the game loop to detect user interactions.

```python
for event in pygame.event.get():
```

```
if event.type == pygame.QUIT:

running = False
```

Blit: Short for "block transfer," this term refers to drawing one surface onto another. In Pygame, you can use the blit() method to display images or sprites on the game window.

```
screen.blit(image_surface, (x, y))
```

Frame Rate (FPS): The number of frames per second that the game displays. Controlling the frame rate is crucial for maintaining a consistent speed for gameplay. Pygame offers pygame.time.Clock() to manage FPS.

Clock: A Pygame object used to control the frame rate of the game. It ensures the game runs at the desired speed across different machines.

Collision Detection: The process of determining when two objects, such as sprites or surfaces, interact with each other. Pygame provides collision detection functions, such as colliderect() and collidepoint().

Tile: A small image or texture used to create the graphical background of a game. Tiles are commonly used in 2D platformers to represent different parts of the game world.

Animation: The process of displaying a sequence of images (frames) over time to create the illusion of movement. In Pygame, animations can be handled by updating the sprite images at regular intervals.

Group: A Pygame object that allows you to manage multiple sprites at once. Sprite groups make it easier to update, draw, and manage large numbers of sprites in a game.

```
all_sprites = pygame.sprite.Group()
```

all_sprites.add(player)

Hitbox: The area of a sprite that can collide with other objects. Hitboxes are often defined using Pygame's Rect object, which simplifies collision detection.

RGB Color Model: A model in which colors are defined by red, green, and blue values. Each value can range from 0 to 255, and colors are represented as tuples (R, G, B) in Pygame.

WHITE = (255, 255, 255)

AI (Artificial Intelligence): Algorithms that control non-player characters (NPCs) in games. AI can range from simple logic for enemy movements to complex decision-making systems.

Understanding these terms will allow you to navigate Pygame's documentation and code more efficiently.

Resources for Further Learning

For those interested in expanding their knowledge beyond the basics, there are numerous resources available that cover various aspects of Python and game development. Here are some recommended avenues for further study:

Official Documentation: One of the best ways to learn more about Pygame and Python is to explore their official documentation. Pygame's official site provides comprehensive guides, tutorials, and references for all its functions and classes. Python's official documentation offers in-depth explanations of its standard libraries, features, and best practices.

Online Tutorials: Websites like Real Python, GeeksforGeeks, and W3Schools offer detailed tutorials on Python and game development topics. These tutorials range from beginner to advanced levels and often include example projects.

Books: There are numerous books on Python game development. "Python Game Programming By Example" by Alejandro Rodas de Paz and "Invent Your Own Computer Games with Python" by Al Sweigart are excellent starting points. These books cover both the basics of Python and more advanced topics in game development using Pygame.

YouTube Channels: Channels like "Tech With Tim" and "freeCodeCamp" offer free, high-quality video tutorials on Python and Pygame. These are great resources for visual learners who prefer hands-on coding demonstrations.

Game Development Communities: Being part of a community can accelerate your learning process. Websites like Stack Overflow, Reddit's game development subreddits, and Discord servers dedicated to game development are invaluable for getting advice, sharing knowledge, and troubleshooting problems.

GitHub Repositories: Reviewing and contributing to open-source Pygame projects on GitHub is a great way to learn how real-world projects are structured. Many developers share their source code, which can be used as learning material or for collaboration.

MOOCs (Massive Open Online Courses): Websites like Coursera, edX, and Udemy offer courses on Python programming and game development. Some courses are free, while others require a fee for certification. These courses often provide structured learning paths and access to knowledgeable instructors.

Coding Challenges: Sites like LeetCode, HackerRank, and CodeWars offer Python-specific coding challenges that can help you improve your problem-solving skills. While these are not directly related to game development, they will improve your understanding of algorithms and data structures, which are crucial for building efficient games.

Local Meetups and Hackathons: Participating in local Python or game development meetups and hackathons is another way to learn. These events offer the chance to collaborate with other developers, work on projects, and receive mentorship.

Blogs and Newsletters: Following game development blogs and subscribing to newsletters can help you stay up-to-date with the latest trends, tools, and techniques in Python game development. Popular blogs include Pygame's official blog, Real Python, and Python Weekly.

By combining these resources with hands-on experience, you can continue to deepen your understanding of Python game development and Pygame.

Sample Projects and Code Snippets

Below are some sample projects and code snippets that can help you get started or provide inspiration for your own game development journey. Each example demonstrates a key concept in Pygame, from basic mechanics to more advanced features.

Simple Game Loop Example

```python
import pygame

pygame.init()

screen = pygame.display.set_mode((640, 480))

running = True

while running:
```

```
for event in pygame.event.get():

if event.type == pygame.QUIT:

running = False

pygame.display.flip()

pygame.quit()
```

This basic game loop is the foundation of any Pygame project. It initializes the Pygame window, listens for events, and updates the screen in a continuous loop until the user closes the window.

Drawing Shapes

```
pygame.draw.rect(screen, (0, 128, 255), pygame.Rect(30, 30, 60, 60))
```

This snippet draws a blue rectangle at the coordinates (30, 30) with a width and height of 60 pixels.

Moving a Sprite with Keyboard Input

```
import pygame

pygame.init()

screen = pygame.display.set_mode((640, 480))

player = pygame.Rect(300, 400, 50, 50)

running = True

while running:

for event in pygame.event.get():

if event.type == pygame.QUIT:
```

```
running = False

keys = pygame.key.get_pressed()

if keys[pygame.K_LEFT]:

player.x -= 5

if keys[pygame.K_RIGHT]:

player.x += 5

screen.fill((0, 0, 0))

pygame.draw.rect(screen, (0, 128, 255), player)

pygame.display.flip()

pygame.quit()
```

This example demonstrates how to move a sprite using keyboard input. The pygame.key.get_pressed() function checks whether a key is being pressed, and based on that input, the player's rectangle will move left or right.

Collision Detection

```
if player.colliderect(enemy):

print("Collision detected!")
```

Here, colliderect() checks whether the player's rectangle has collided with the enemy's rectangle, printing a message if a collision occurs.

Playing Sound

```
import pygame
```

pygame.mixer.init()

pygame.mixer.music.load('background.mp3')

pygame.mixer.music.play(-1)

This snippet demonstrates how to load and play background music in a Pygame project. The play(-1) method ensures that the music loops indefinitely.

These code snippets and sample projects serve as building blocks for more complex games.

Pygame & Python API Reference Guide

Below is a reference guide to some of the most commonly used Pygame and Python APIs for game development. This guide is not exhaustive, but it will cover the essential functions and methods you'll need in most Pygame projects.

Pygame Functions

pygame.init(): Initializes all Pygame modules.

pygame.display.set_mode(): Creates the game window with the specified resolution.

pygame.event.get(): Returns a list of all events that have occurred since the last call.

pygame.quit(): Shuts down all Pygame modules.

pygame.time.Clock(): Creates a clock object that can be used to manage the frame rate.

Drawing Functions

pygame.draw.rect(): Draws a rectangle on the screen.

pygame.draw.circle(): Draws a circle on the screen.

pygame.draw.line(): Draws a line between two points.

Image and Sound

pygame.image.load(): Loads an image from a file.

pygame.mixer.init(): Initializes the Pygame sound mixer.

pygame.mixer.Sound(): Loads a sound effect.

Input Handling

pygame.key.get_pressed(): Returns a list of key states.

pygame.mouse.get_pos(): Returns the current position of the mouse.

Collision Detection

pygame.Rect.colliderect(): Checks if two rectangles are colliding.

pygame.sprite.Group(): Creates a group of sprites.

This reference guide will be helpful for quickly finding and using key Pygame and Python functions while developing your games.

Frequently Asked Questions

How do I install Pygame?

To install Pygame, you can use Python's package manager, pip. Simply run the following command in your terminal or command prompt:

pip install pygame

Make sure you have Python installed and set up in your system before running this command.

What version of Python do I need for Pygame?

Pygame supports Python 3.7 and later versions. It's recommended to use the latest stable version of Python to ensure compatibility with modern libraries and features.

Can I use Pygame for 3D games?

Pygame is primarily designed for 2D games. While it's possible to create basic 3D games using external libraries or custom algorithms, Pygame is not optimized for 3D graphics. If you're interested in 3D game development, you may want to explore libraries like Panda3D or engines like Unity.

Is Pygame suitable for mobile game development?

Pygame is not designed for mobile platforms out of the box. It is more suited for desktop applications. However, there are ways to port Pygame games to mobile platforms using additional tools like Kivy or Pyjs. Keep in mind that this may require additional effort and modification of your code.

Can I integrate Pygame with other Python libraries?

Yes, Pygame can be easily integrated with other Python libraries, including NumPy for advanced mathematics, PIL (Pillow) for image processing, and even libraries like OpenCV for computer vision tasks. Pygame is very flexible and can be extended with external libraries.

How do I handle different screen resolutions?

To handle different screen resolutions, you can design your game to be resolution-independent. One way to achieve this is by scaling your game's graphics dynamically based on the screen size. You can get the user's screen resolution using pygame.display.Info() and adjust your game window and graphics accordingly.

What is the best way to optimize Pygame performance?

To optimize performance in Pygame, you should aim to:

- Minimize the number of surfaces being updated every frame.

- Use hardware-accelerated surfaces where possible.

- Keep your game logic efficient by avoiding unnecessary calculations in the game loop.

- Use sprite groups to batch updates and rendering for multiple objects.

How do I package my game for distribution?

You can package your Pygame project as a standalone executable using tools like PyInstaller or cx_Freeze. These tools bundle your Python code and all necessary dependencies into a single file that can be executed without requiring users to install Python or Pygame.

Can I use Pygame for professional game development?

While Pygame is a fantastic tool for learning game development and building small to medium-sized projects, it may not be suitable for large-scale, commercial games due to its limitations in 3D rendering, performance, and mobile support. However, many successful indie games have been developed using Pygame.

Where can I find Pygame tutorials and resources?

There are many online resources to help you get started with Pygame. The official Pygame documentation is a great place to begin. Additionally, websites like Real Python, Tech With Tim (YouTube), and GeeksforGeeks offer step-by-step tutorials. For more in-depth learning, books like "Invent Your Own Computer Games with Python" by Al Sweigart are highly recommended.

How do I add physics to my Pygame project?

For simple physics, you can implement gravity, collisions, and object movement directly in your game logic. For more advanced physics simulations, you can use external libraries like PyMunk or integrate Box2D with Pygame. These libraries provide robust physics engines to handle complex interactions and mechanics.